AF600038

CATHOLIC UNIVERSITY OF AMERICA
CANON LAW STUDIES
No. XLIV

CANON 6

or

The Relation of the Codex Juris Canonici to Preceding Legislation

A DISSERTATION

Submitted to the Faculty of Canon Law of the Catholic University of America in partial fulfillment of the requirements for the Degree of

DOCTOR OF CANON LAW

by

REV. NICOLAS J. NEUBERGER

CATHOLIC UNIVERSITY OF AMERICA
WASHINGTON, D. C.
1927

Nihil Obstat:

✠ Thomas J. Shahan,

Censor Deputatus.

Washingtonii, D. C. die 10 Maii, 1927.

Imprimatur:

✠ Michael J. Curley,

Archiepiscopus Baltimorensis.

Baltimorae, die 10 Maii, 1927.

CONTENTS

INTRODUCTION.

The keynote of the Code is change. The external technique of the Decretals is supplanted by the modern form of civil codes. In the internal technique many opportune alterations abound. The "Arduum sane munus" of Pius X made these forecasts and the introductory clause of Canon 6 manifests their reality. Much of the former discipline is also retained in the Code. Legislation effective for centuries could not be thrust aside with due prudence. Many enactments are a restatement of or have affinity with the divine laws. The codifiers kept such legislation substantially intact. The terminology, however, was made conformable to the structure of Canons.

The change of law, as all changes, ever implies two terms: the "*terminus a quo*" and the "*terminus ad quem.*" The "*terminus ad quem*" is the Benedictine Code, and the pertinent legislation antecedent to the Code is the "*terminus a quo.*" The purpose of this dissertation is to show the relation of the two terms, be it expressed by way of contrast or similarity. In chronological order the relevant sources of the former discipline are presented. The principles which govern the internal technique comprise the greater part of the dissertation. To detect the determinants of abrogation, to cite rules of interpretation where the old is recast into Canons, to proffer Hermeneutics where the old and new legislation meet, to establish criteria where there is a doubtful discrepancy in laws, these, in fine, propose the scope of the writer.

CHAPTER I.

THE PRE-CODE *"DISCIPLINA VIGENS."*

"Disciplina vigens" is the ecclesiastical legislation promulgated and enforced by competent authority. The pre-code *"disciplina vigens"* is the legislation which was effective before the promulgation of the Code. To determine the extension of the former discipline is imperative in the study of Canon 6. The relation of the old law to the new postulates an adequate research in both periods of legislation. The pre-code discipline in time and in subject-matter covers an enormous field. It is useless, therefore, to expect an historical treatise on each law. Likewise, it would be presumptuous to anticipate a syllabus of abiding laws which have weathered the principles of abrogation. The study of the pre-code discipline is confined to the sources of the old law. Some additional reflections are made on the principles of abrogation and retention. In fine, the purpose at hand is to disclose where the old law may be found and how to determine whether it is abrogated or not. Furthermore, the theme is restricted to the common general law.

ARTICLE I. THE "DISCIPLINA VIGENS"

Antecedent to and in the *"Corpus Juris Canonici."*

Generally, the history of Canon Law is divided into three periods: 1) *"Jus Antiquum"* dating from the beginning of the Church to the time of Gratian (intra ann. 1140-50); 2) *"Jus Novum"* from Gratian to the Council of Trent (1545-63); 3) *"Jus Novissimum"* from the Council of Trent to our time.[1] In the present survey there is no need of adhering to this traditional division.

---

1 Gasparri, *Praefatio Codicis Juris Canonici,* XIX.

The task at hand is to disclose the relevant sources of the "*disciplina vigens.*" For convenience, the writer has made the "*Corpus Juris Canonici*" the dividing point. The "*Corpus Juris Canonici,*" in two of its collections, the Gregorian Decretals and the Decretals of Boniface VIII, manifests the first attempts of abrogating other collections. Another reason may be added why the "*Corpus Juris Canonici*" is the center of the division. The "*Rex Pacificus*" of Gregory IX has caused not a little trouble in determining the extension of the "*disciplina vigens.*"

Of old, wholesale abrogation of laws was unknown. There were, however, some partial annulments, but they were infrequent. Usually, the Bull of promulgation of the new law qualified the ablation of antecedent legislation. The "*Rex Pacificus*" of Gregory IX and the "*Sacrosanctae*" of Boniface VIII are notable examples. Ordinarily, a principle of relative exclusion was uttered which debarred from the common general law specified collections and constitutions. Furthermore, certain accepted principles on the relation of individual laws were applied by jurists. Equally competent legislators could abrogate antecedent contradictory laws. The introduction of an enactment "*ipso facto*" annulled a preceding contrary law.

With these prefatory observations at hand the process of determining the "*disciplina vigens*" and its embrace now ensues. One way of ascertaining, and, it seems, the shortest, what sources are legitimate, is by showing the illegitimate. Since the Decretals of Gregory IX is the first collection in the history of Canon Law to which some official abrogation is attached, it is reasonable to begin with this work. What abrogatory force has the "*Rex Pacificus*" of Gregory? Did Gregory make void all antecedent legislation? If there was only a partial abrogation, what was discarded?

No one concedes that the "*Rex Pacificus*" kept intact all prior laws. All authors agree that Gregory annulled the "*Compilatio I Bernardi Papiensis*" (c. 1190), the

Compilatio II Joannis Walensis" (c. 1200), *"Compilatio III Innocentii III"* (1198-1216), *"Compilatio"* IV (c. 1216), and the *"Compilatio V Honorii III"* (1226). Some jurists are more venturesome. Augustine, Laurin and Schulte consider the legislation antecedent and subsequent to the *"Decretum Gratiani"* effete, whenever it is not embodied in the *"Decretum Gratiani"* nor in the Gregorian Decretals.[2] Why the Gratian Decree remains unmolested whilst other kindred collections are substantially abrogated is difficult to fathom. Certainly it is not conclusively proven by these authors.

For the sake of brevity, five authors have been selected as representatives of explanations on the abrogatory force of the *"Rex Pacificus."* Wernz advocates an abrogation of the decretals collected after the Gratian Decree.[3] Without advancing reasons, Augustine considers the Gregorian Decretals "the Code of Law for the universal (Latin) Church, to the exclusion of all others of a general character. But this collection did not abrogate either the Decretum Gratiani or existing particular laws."[4] The third class sponsored by Laurin maintains the same attitude but with inconclusive arguments.[5] In an obscure way Schulte suggests the same range, but confines the subject-matter to the Decretals.[6] Maroto avers that all preceding collections of Decretals were abrogated. The Gratian Decree, however, is an exception. There was not, as it seems, an annulment of all general laws not contained in the *Decretum* or in the Gregorian Decretals.[7]

Wernz assumes that the Gratian Decree is left untouched by Gregory. The decretals collected since Gra-

---

2 Augustine, *A Commentary of Canon Law,* Vol. I, p. 37.; Schulte, *Geschichte der Quellen und Literatur des canonischen Rechts,* Band 2, p. 16; Laurin, *Introductio in Corpus Juris Canonici,* p. 148.

3 Wernz, *Jus Decretalium,* Vol. I, p. 363.

4 Augustine, loc. cit.

5 Laurin, op. cit., p. 146.

6 Schulte, loc. cit.

7 Maroto, *Institutiones Juris Canonici,* Tomus I, p. 75.

tian, he continues, are considered null and void. Wernz fails to mention the nature of the decretals. The legislative enactments subsequent to the Gratian Decree are commonly limited to the five compilations. These compilations contained not only decretalistic letters but also constitutions, as is evinced from the Bull *"Rex Pacificus."*

The absence of arguments in Augustine's theory may be attributed to the nature of the work. His history of Canon Law is a compendium, and not an exhaustive treatise. The footnotes to his statements, however, warrant a classification with Laurin. Two reasons are alleged by Laurin which guarantee immunity to the Gratian Decree: 1) Bernardus Papiensis and Joannes Galensis considered their works merely a complement to the Gratian Decree and, therefore, its abrogation is unwarranted; 2) Gregory wanted to displace the compilations alone. The mere opinion of two compilers does not advance an argument for the inviolability of the Gratian Decree. The second reason is a statement of truth; but it is not substantiated by arguments based on the *"Rex Pacificus."*

What is the juridical value of laws antedating the Gratian Decree? Laurin avers that these are abrogated because the two compilers, Bernardus Papiensis and Joannes Galensis, considered them useless in the ecclesiastical forum. The Decretals of Gregory supplanted the compilations. Therefore, he concludes, all legislation not embodied in the Decretum Gratiani and the Decretals are destitute of juridical appraisal.[8] It seems logical to assert that the private, unauthentic, unofficial utterances remain personal opinions. The second part is hopelessly irreconcilable. Two compilers deemed the legislation antecedent to Gratian obsolete. The Gregorian Decretals crystallized their collections as also their opinions. Therefore, whatever the compilers conjectured on a cer-

8 Laurin, op. cit., p. 145, 147, seq.

tain matter is approved by Gregory; for, he used their works as sources for the Decretals. Surely a *"non sequitur"* is the label for this form of argumentation.

Schulte is representative of a fourth theory. He argues rightly that the five compilations are identified with the word *"volumen"* as expressly used in the Bull of promulgation. The collection of Gregory was further directed to the compilation of the Decretals and the Constitutions not embodied in the five compilations. It was also extended to the juridical output of Gregory prior to the promulgation of the Decretals. Here enters Schulte's inconclusive *ergo*. Therefore, the *"Decretum Gratiani"* is immune from the principles of abrogation as proclaimed in the *"Rex Pacificus."*[9] The term *"Decretum Gratiani"* is not found in the premises but is mysteriously inserted into the conclusion. In a later portion of his work, Schulte seems to limit the abrogation to the decretals. When the *"Rex Pacificus"* was published the Decretals not found in the Gratian Decree nor in the Decretals of Gregory lost their juridical status. No word on the constitutions is disclosed.[10] Time and again he insists that the *"Jus commune"* is the sole consideration. Does he identify decretals with constitutions, or does the common law include both the decretals and the constitutions? Whatever the reply may be, no reasons have been alleged why the Gratian Decree has been untouched and other private collections have been abolished. Schulte has catalogued the sources from which Gregory compiled the Decretals. The sources are predominantly confined to the five compilations. The abrogatory force of the *"Rex Pacificus"* is restricted to the sources of the Gregorian Decretals. This argument assures immunity to the Gratian Decree, but it does not declare that other private collections are abolished. Schulte seems to assume, rather than prove the questions. Thus far, it is unfounded that Gregory abolished all decretals and con-

---

9 Schulte, op. cit., Band 2, p. 8.
10 Schulte, op. cit., Band 2, p. 16.

stitutions not found in the "*Decretum*" and in the Decretals of Gregory.[11]

Without adducing reasons or quoting authorities Maroto[12] acclaims null and void all collections preceding the Gregorian Decretals. Why the author has confined his observations to the decretals is difficult to fathom. The "*Rex Pacificus*" explicitly mentions both constitutions and decretals. The Gratian Decree, however, is not abrogated. Why the Decretum Gratiani is juridically inviolable whilst other kindred collections are abrogated is not ascertained by Maroto.

Have some collections survived the principle of exclusion as found in the "*Rex Pacificus?*" What works have been abrogated? What is the extension of the ablation? These are questions still unsolved. Perchance a study of the "*Rex Pacificus,*" with suggestions from the five authors enumerated above, will advance an approximation in solving the questions.

To quote the "*Rex Pacificus*" in its entirety is useless. The pertinent paragraph is reproduced here in its most essential parts:

> *Sane diversas constitutiones et decretales epistolas praedecessorum nostrorum, in diversa dispersas volumina, quarum aliquae propter nimiam similitudinem, et quaedam propter contrarietatem, nonnullae etiam propter sui prolixitatem, confusionem inducere videbantur, aliquae vero vagabantur extra volumina supra dicta, quae tanquam incertae frequenter in judiciis vacillabant, . . . illas in unum volumen resecatis superfluis providimus redigendas, adjicientes constitutiones nostras et decretales epistolas, per quas nonnulla, quae in prioribus erant dubia, declarantur.*[13]

The words "*diversas constitutiones et decretales epistolas.....in diversa dispersas volumina*" point to specific works known to Gregory. It is commonly conceded that the five compilations are identified with the "*diversa*

11 Scherer, *Handbuch des Kirchenrechtes*, Teil I, p. 251; Wernz, op. cit., p. 363, footnote.

12 Maroto, op. cit., p. 75.

13 "*Corpus Juris Canonici,*" Vol. II, p. 1.

volumina." Schulte proffers a chart which shows in a general way, that the five compilations are the volumes mentioned by Gregory.[14] Laurin suggests no more than a traditional opinion. His observations are the same as Schulte.[15] The word *"illas"* seems of utmost importance in the interpretation of the *"Rex Pacificus." "Illas,"* those, that is, the former, must be redacted into one volume (*"in unum volumen redigendas"*). *"Illas,"* the former, refers to those constitutions and decretalistic letters befuddled with undue similarity, contrariety and prolixity. These ought to constitute the bulk of the sources for the Gregorian Decretals. Thereby the legislator points out the sources from which the superfluous were cut asunder (*"resecatis superfluis"*). Then the residue is merged into one volume which is called *"Decretales Gregorii IX."* Whatever comprised the sources of the *"Decretales Gregorii IX"* is abrogated. A survey of the sources testifies to the extent of the abrogation. The Friedberg-Richter edition of the *"Corpus Juris Canonici"* has a table of sources from which the Gregorian Decretals were compiled.[16] It would be cumbersome to cite the statistics contained therein. A research reveals that the mass redounds to the five compilations. It may be legitimately concluded that the compilations enumerated above are alone supplanted by the Gregorian Decretals.

The *"Rex Pacificus"* continues: *"aliquae vero vagabantur extra volumina supra dicta, quae tanquam incertae frequenter in judiciis vacillabant."* It seems these words allude to the constitutions and decretalistic letters of Gregory. His enactments certainly were not included in these five compilations (*"extra volumina supradicta"*). Another argument to prop this assertion is found in the two phrases: *"extra volumina supra dicta, quae tanquam incertae frequenter in judiciis vacillabant"*

14 Schulte, op. cit., Band 2, p. 8, seq.

15 Laurin, op. cit., p. 147.

16 *Corpus Juris Canonici,* Vol. II, p. XI, seq.

and "*adjicientes constitutiones nostras et decretales epistolas, per quas nonnulla, quae in prioribus erant dubia.*" The legislation "*extra volumina supra dicta*" was used with uncertainty in judicial processes. To the same class Gregory adds his constitutions and decretalistic letters, some of which were doubtful. The "*incertae*" in the first clause corresponds to the word "*dubia*" at the end of the paragraph. The phrase "*aliquae vero vagabantur,*" etc., may refer to other collections which were used as accessorial sources to the Gregorian Decretals, e.g., "*Canones Apostolorum,*" conciliar enactments and the like.

The prohibition at the end of the "*Rex Pacificus*" is directed to a compilation of the same matter. Hereafter the approbation of the Holy See is required for any edition of the Gregorian Decretals. Other pontiffs thruout the centuries have issued kindred prohibitions.

The argument has been advanced that the five compilations alone were annulled by the "*Rex Pacificus*" of Gregory IX. It is evident that a principle of general exclusion cannot be extorted from the document. Nor can the allegation be made that the Gratian Decree is the only private collection outside of the five compilations which has not been abrogated. It is immune from the principles of abrogation to the same degree as other private collections antedating it. The general laws embodied in the private collections have the same juridical value as they had in their original source, from which they were gleaned.

"*De Jure,*" as the legitimate sources indicate, the "*disciplina vigens*" of this period is the common general law not included in the five compilations. It excludes enactments corrected "*nominatim*" in the Gregorian Decretals. Furthermore, it discards all antecedent legislation which is contradictory. "*De facto,*" however, the surviving laws may have been confined to the "*Decretum Gratiani*" and the "*Decretales Gregorii IX.*" Whatever the custom may have been at the time is difficult to understand. This juridical element has ever been recognized in the history of Canon Law. The only available information which restricts the sources of Canon Law to the Gratian Decree and the Gregorian Decretals is the statement of the two compilers mentioned above.

As a matter of fact, however, some general laws could be found outside of the "*Decretum Gratiani*" and the "*Decretales Gregorii IX.*" Several arguments may be adduced to verify this statement. The "*Fontes Juris Canonici*" supplies conciliar and papal acts which are not found in the Gratian Decree, nor in the Decretals, or rather more specifically not found in the "*Corpus Juris Canonici.*"[17] The "*Collectio Dionysio-Hadriana*" a quasi-authentic collection[18] is not recorded in the sources of the Gregorian Decretals.[19] This collection had many general laws which to all appearances had never been revoked. The many "*Bullaria*" have Constitutions and Acts of the pontiffs which are not embodied in Gratian Decree and the Gregorian Decretals. These had the force of universal law which had not been declared null and void.[20] When Febronianism and Gallicanism wrought havoc in their respective countries some French jurists were bent on disvaluing the "*Corpus Juris Canonici*" to attain their sinister purposes. Therefore, they attributed juridical value to the "*Collectio Hadriana*" alone.[21] This may point to the fact that the "*Collectio Hadriana*" still survived side by side with the collections recently promulgated. From these testimonies it may be inferred that not a few laws were extant which antedated the "*Decretum Gratiani.*" Likewise, it is logical to conclude that private collections prior to the Gratian Decree were as immune from the principles of abrogation as the Gratian Decree.

---

17 *Codicis Juris Canonici Fontes*, Prooemium VI.

18 Maroto, op. cit., p. 59.

19 *Corpus Juris Canonici*, Vol. II, p. XI, seq.

20 Maroto, op. cit., p. 90.

21 Bernereggi, *Methodi E Sistemi Delle Antiche Collezione E Del Nuovo Codice Di Diritto Canonico*, p. 88.

Thus far, the five compilations are juridically obliterated. Other general laws not contradicted by subsequent legislation are left intact.[22] The Decretals of Gregory, in their dispositive parts, have the force of universal law. Advancing in this study of the "*disciplina vigens*" the next official, authentic collection is the *Decretales Bonifatii VIII*. The work was officially promulgated by the Bull "*Sacrosanctae.*"[23] The Decretals of Boniface, also called "*Liber Sextus,*" contain the collections of individual Roman Pontiffs, chiefly, Innocent IV, Alexander IV, Urban IV, Clement IV, Gregory X and Nicolas III.[24] Some material was also taken from the Decretals of Gregory and the first and second Councils of Lyons (1245, 1274 respectively).[25] What principles of abrogation were promulgated by the Bull "*Sacrosanctae?*" The enactments of Boniface made before the "*Liber Sextus*" are not abrogated even if they are not included in the work. All laws, however, published after the Decretals of Gregory which are not inserted in the "*Liber Sextus*" or especially reserved, are ablated. Furthermore, Boniface excludes all universal laws contrary to the enactments of his work even if they are contained in the collection of Gregory IX.[26] The Decretals of Gregory and Boniface were the first and the last collections which had a principle of exclusion attached to them. True, other authentic collections will follow; no work, however, will be found warranting an abrogation of preceding collections.

In chronological order the "*Clementinae*" follow the Decretals of Boniface the VIII. These were published only a few years later. Several constitutions of the predecessors of Clement and the Council of Vienne (France 1313) originally comprised the subject-matter. The collection was not published by Clement V. After a

---

22 Wernz, op. cit., p. 363.
23 *Corpus Juris Canonici*, Vol. II, p. 934.
24 Phillips, op. cit., p. 70.
25 Augustine, op. cit., Vol. I, p. 39.
26 Maroto, op. cit., Vol. I, p. 78.

notable revision it was promulgated by John XXII in 1317.[27] No clause invalidating any other collections is found in the Bull of Promulgation. The general law not embodied in the "*Clementinae*" retains its initial value. It is classified juridically with other authentic collections. The abiding principle of contradiction would alone qualify the preceding legislation.

Contrarywise, the "*Extravagantes*" of John XXII and the "*Extravagantes Communes*" are not authentic collections. Their legal worth is confined to a private, unauthentic compilation, as the "*Decretum Gratiani.*" Their presence in the "*Corpus Juris Canonici*" adds not a particle of authenticity. The collection as a mere compilation has no juridical value. The private collectanea only reprints the former law. Whatever its primary estimate may have been, it remains unchanged in these individual collections.

Thus far, the "*disciplina vigens*" is found in the official collections of Gregory the IX, Boniface the VIII, and the "*Clementinae*" promulgate by John XXII.

Article II.—"Disciplina Vigens"

Subsequent to the "*Corpus Juris Canonici.*"

In the foregoing paragraphs the legislation antecedent to and in the *Corpus Juris Canonici* has been surveyed. The authentic collections were segregated from the private works. The principle of abrogation relative to certain collections has been explained and applied in detail. This period, dating from the "*Corpus Juris Canonici,*" has no authentic collectanea which abolish other collections. The term of this division is the "*Codex Juris Canonici.*"

The first source of the discipline subsequent to the "*Corpus Juris Canonici*" was the "*Regulae Cancellariae Apostolicae.*" These regulations were divided into three classes: 1) the directive which never constituted a com-

27 "*Quoniam Nulla,*" *Corpus Juris Canonici,* Vol. II, p. 1130.

mon universal law, 2) the judicial, and, 3) the reserved had the juridical force of universal law *"sede apostolica non vacante."* [28] Schmalzgrueber contrary to Cocchi assigns convincing reasons why the *"Regulae"* are not classified with universal law. They are local constitutions instituted by the Roman Chancery. The *"Regulae"* lose their binding force on the death of the pontiff. Therefore, they cannot be universal law; for universal laws of their nature are stable.[29]

Conciliar acts added not a little to the deposit of legislation. The Babylonian Captivity and its logical sequel the Great Western Schism caused much disturbance in the Church. Councils were opened and sessions held without the necessary official approbation. It was, therefore, overwhelmingly difficult to ascertain what acts were authentic and what acts were spurious. The Council of Pisa held in 1409 gave birth to unofficial acts and decrees [30] which have been quoted freely and undisputedly by canonists.[31] Sessions 42, 43, 44, 45 were legitimately convoked by Martin V.[32] Martin V did not exclude disciplinary decrees in the Council though many emphasize the contrary.[33]

All the decrees of the Council of Basle (1437-1443) from session XXV to XLV inclusive, are fictitious and invalid.[34] Eugene IV (1431-1447) convoked the Council of Ferrara-Florence. All the disciplinary decrees of this gathering have the highest sanction. The legitimate sessions of Basle and all the sessions of Ferrara-Florence are termed the Seventh General Council.[35]

---

28 Cocchi, *Commentarium in Codicem Juris Canonici,* Vol. I, p. 32; *"Sapienti Consilio,"* July 29, 1908, and the *"Romanae Curiae,"* Dec. 8, 1910, made some slight changes.

29 Schmalzgrueber, *Jus Ecclesiasticum Universum,* Vol. I, p. 158.

30 Funk, *Manual of Church History,* Vol. II, p. 15.

31 Hergenroether-Kirsch, *Handbuch der Allgemeinen Kirchengeschichte,* p. 833, seq.

32 Hergenroether-Kirsch, op. cit., p. 870, seq.

33 Funk, op. cit., p. 18.

34 Hefele, *Conciliengeschichte,* Vol. IX, p. 445; Hergenroether-Kirsch, op. cit., 903, seq.

35 Funk, op. cit., Vol. II, p. 24.

The Council of Trent (1545-1563) is viewed as an epoch-making event in the history of Canon Law. The disciplinary decrees constituted a real code of ecclesiastical law.[36] Many sessions were divided into parts; the first being doctrinal whilst the second was disciplinary. The latter usually was captioned *"Decretum de Reformatione."* The second part of the sessions 5, 6, 7, 13, 14, 21, 22, 23 with both parts of sessions 24 and 25 produce the legislation of Trent. With the exception of the *"Tametsi"* the disciplinary enactments of Trent were promulgated by Pius IV in the *"Benedictus Deus,"* January 26, 1564. The laws became effective the first of the following May. The dispositive parts alone have a juridical status. Annotations found in some of the collections of the Council of Trent warrant no legal value; for these are merely the interpretative aids of private authors. Under the most severe penalties Pius IV prohibited private commentaries and annotations on the disciplinary decrees of Trent. The Sacred Congregation of the Council was instituted for the purpose of interpreting the acts of the Council.[37] The common law legitimately remained unchanged save the customs, universal or particular, changed them.[38]

What are the notable collections of these conciliar acts. The first attempts of compiling the acts of the general councils were made in the 16th and 17th centuries. The principal collectors were Jacob Merlin, Peter Crabbe, Lawrence Surio, Severus Binio, and Jacob Sirmond. The outstanding collectanea comes from John Dominic Mansi with the title *"Sacrorum Conciliorum Nova et Amplissima Collectio."* The work contains 78 volumes, thirty-one of which were under the personal supervision of Mansi and the remainder was finished by others.

Hand in hand with these come the constitutions and the acts of the Roman Pontiffs. Very complete collections

---

36 Vermeersch-Creusen, *Epitome Juris Canonici*, Vol. I, p. 21.

37 Maroto, op. cit., p. 88.

38 Wernz, op. cit., p. 380.

of this part of the "*disciplina vigens*" are accessible. These compilations are commonly called "*Bullaria.*" Of prominence is the "*Bullarium Cherubini,*" composed by Laertes Cherubini in 1586. This comprised the acts of the Pontiffs from Gregory VII to Sixtus V. Later it was extended from Leo I to Paul V. This again had additions from his son. Again in 1672 Angelo de Lantusca and Paulo de Roma made valuable annexations. Another notable collection is the "*Magnum Bullarium Romanum*" or as more commonly called "*Bullarium Romanum Luxemburgense.*" This collection contains acts of the pontiffs from Leo I to Benedict XIV.[39] Carl Cocquelines contributed "*Bullarum Privilegiorum, ac Diplomatum Romanorum Pontificum Amplissima Collectio*" which embodies juridical matter dating from Leo I to Clement XII.[40] The "*Bullarii Romani Continuatio*" embraced the constitutions dating from Clement XIII to Pius VIII inclusive. This canonical treasure was a collaboration of Andrew Barberi and Alexander Spetia.[41] The famous canonist Aloysius Tomassetti edited the "*Bullarium Taurinense*" which includes pontifical acts from Leo I to Clement XIII.[42] "*Bullarium Diplomatum et Privilegiorum Sanctorum Romanorum Pontificum*" the last of this series was produced by Francisco Gaude.[43] These collections as well as the conciliar collectanea peremptorily remain private works.

The "*Bullarium Benedicti XIV*" was omitted in the chronological order on account of a character distinct from the aforementioned. Authenticity marks this collection. It embraces the constitutions of his six predecessors as also his own constitutions. Many of the personal acts of Benedict are not endowed with universality. These acts of particular legislation come down to us with the common general law. To extricate the former

---

39 Luxemburg, 1727, Vol. 19.
40 Rome, 1762, 14 tomes.
41 Rome, 1835-57, Vol. 18.
42 Turin, 1875, Vol. 24.
43 Augustae Taurinorum, 1875.

from the latter is one of the difficulties of interpreting and finding the exact "*disciplina vigens.*"[44]

Now, the collections closer to our times will be summarily viewed. Anthony Bernasconi left as his heritage to Canon Law the collections of the Acts of Gregory XVI. Select acts, which he deemed useful to canonical science, constituted the body of the work.[45]

The Acts of the later pontiffs, commonly called "*Acta Apud Sanctam Sedem,*" in reality had the title "*Acta ex iis Decerpta Quae Apud Sanctam Sedem.*" Marietti was commissioned to print this work. Pius IX, the then reigning pontiff, favored him with this privilege. That it is destitute of authenticity is gleaned from the words of Pius IX, "*neque volumus silentio praeterire, ne quis in errorem inducatur, hoc qualecumque opus nulla publica auctoritate fulcire.*"[46] Later the title was changed to "*Acta Sanctae Sedis.*" This transition was effected by Peter Avanzini, namely in volumes VI and VII.[47] Volumes VIII, and IX are attributed to Zitelli.[48] Joseph Pennacchi and Victor Piazzesi are the authors of volumes X to XX; whilst volumes XXI to XXVI inclusive are ascribed to Piazzesi alone.[49] The "*Acta Sanctae Sedis*" was pronounced official and authentic by Pius X, May 23, 1904.[50] In 1909 came the "*Acta Apostolicae Sedis*" which even to date remains the official commentary of the Holy See.[51]

A study of the collections of the various congregations is not a little interesting. The first in order is the Congregation of the Council. Its representative collection is the "*Thesaurus Resolutionum S. C. Concilii.*" It has the status of a quasi-official collection. In sober truth it means nothing but a private collectanea; for, it pro-

---

44 Maroto, op. cit., p. 92.
45 Maroto, loc. cit.
46 Acta Apud Sanctam Sedem, Rome, Vol. I, 1865, p. 6.
47 Acta Sanctae Sedis, Rome, Vol. VI, 1870, p. 2.
48 Acta Sanctae Sedis, Rome, Vol. X (title) 1873.
49 Acta Sanctae Sedis, Rome, Vol. XXXVII, 1904.
50 Acta Sanctae Sedis, Rome, Vol. XXXVII, 1904.
51 Acta Apostolicae Sedis, Rome, Vol. I, 1909.

ceeded from the Secretary of the congregation. The work was begun by Lambertini, later known as the illustrious Benedict XIV. When the compilation ended in 1908 it numbered 167 volumes. The annual accretion to the Thesaurus ceased in 1908, the year in which the official commentary of the Holy See became its substitute.[52]

The "*Collectanea in usum Secretariae S. C. Episcoporum et Regularium*" was the private work of Andrew Bizarri. The first volumes appeared in 1863 and were augmented by a second edition in 1886.

In 1907 there appeared the invaluable collections of the "*Collectanea Sacrae Congregationis De Propaganda Fide*" Therein are aligned in chronological order the decrees of the Congregation, and also the papal constitutions affecting the missionary countries. Juridical matters within the competency of other congregations and pertaining to countries under the Propaganda are also included. This collection has no more than private value.[53]

The "*Decreta Authentica Congregationis Sacrorum Rituum*" is an authentic collection. It was arranged in collective form by Gardelini. Later it was altered and approved by the same congregation. Leo XIII finally gave it the official character which is attached to it today.

These are the sources of general law antecedent to the Code. By disclosing the principle of exclusion some very few canonical collections were discarded. These generic observations are destined to aid the canonist in finding the "*disciplina vigens*" in the old legislation. The segregation of the authentic from the private collections has little practical value. The former adds a security which is absent in the latter. For all purposes the two are used indiscriminately by canonists. Moreover the principle of contradiction has been insisted on in the course of this study. It remains, however, for the individual canonist to detect this conflict in all forms of legislation.

---

52 Maroto, op. cit., p. 94.

53 Rome, 1907.

ARTICLE III. THE STATUS OF THE "DISCIPLINA VIGENS."

The status of preceding legislation was pathetically confusing. The multiplicity of laws amply portrays the status. Spontaneously canonists described the legislation antecedent to the code as "*immensum aliarum super alias coarcervatarum legum cumulum.*" Innumerable enactments were obsolete and long abrogated. These, however, were launched in collections side by side with the "*disciplina vigens.*" This turmoil was increased by the imperfection of the orders used in the collections. Some were arranged in chronological order, others were systematically aligned, withal quite imperfect.[54]

Were one to trace a law, obstacles without number would be present. The enactment under consideration was found either in authentic or private collections. If the latter, supreme caution must be exercised by the canonist. Then the existence of the law must be challenged. Was it abrogated? Had it been contradicted by a subsequent enactment? When immunity from ablation is assured then the jurist must determine whether the law is universal or particular. If it is particular, then it is utterly discarded; if general, the narrative must be separated from the dispositive part. In the decretals it was a huge task to extricate the real law; for these were originally responses to particular cases. In the constitutions the prolix, metaphorical style made it difficult to find the dispositive portion of laws.

Useless repetition, obscurities, and contrarieties abounded. In addition, silence on many points of law caused not a little controversy among the jurists. In such cases the canonists had recourse to Roman Law, or to custom, or to the opinions of the doctors, in extreme instances even to particular law.[55]

The Postulates of the Vatican Council aid not a little in painting the condition of the laws prior to the Code. Laws of yester-century are not always adapted to suc-

---

54 DeMeester, *Compendium Juris Canonici,* Vol. I, p. 49.
55 *Codex Juris Canonici,* Preface XXIII.

ceeding years. There were laws which were scarcely observed. The Vatican Fathers asked for a repeal of the law of fast and abstinence to avoid scandal; for, this precept of the church was scarcely observed and not a few thought a general dispensation prevailed.[56]

Marriage legislation could have sponsored some mitigation. The Fathers of the Vatican requested a diminution of diriment impediments. Repeated appeals were made to lower the degrees of consanguinity and affinity; for colonization with its frequent change of domicile unduly protracted the necessary investigations.[57] Impractical inquisitions on which the validity of dispensations depended also abounded. On the score of nullity some dispensations demanded revelations of personal turpitude. This made life unpleasant for the priest and spiritually hazardous for the penitent.[58] There was also an urge for greater episcopal power over matrimonial dispensations. This was requested to offset the long delays, the interminable juridical processes used in verifying the motives for the dispensation, and also the uncertainty in establishing valid causes for dispensations.[59]

The Fathers of the Vatican also complained that the juridical processes varied too much in diverse localities. A very strong appeal was made to adopt uniformity in the judicial courts and to abolish prescriptions no longer tolerated by the law. These few paragraphs expose, in a summary, the status of the "*disciplina vigens*" antecedent to the Code. No body of men could make more wholesome suggestions than the Fathers of the Vatican Council.

---

[56] Martin, *Omnium Concilii Vaticani Documentorum Collectio*, p. 191.
[57] op. cit., p. 176.
[58] loc. cit.
[59] op. cit., pp. 176, 177, 186, 191.

CHAPTER II.

THE CODE.

The *"Codex Juris Canonici Pii X Pontificis Maximi Iussu Digestus Benedicti Papae XV Auctoritate Promulgatus"* is the greatest accomplishment of the century. The stupendous task of collaborating and codifying has been overwhelmingly successful. Jurists were loath to encourage the undertaking, fearful of failure.[1] But undaunted the codifiers began the task. The alignment of innumerable sources in which conflicting and obsolete laws thrived, the segregation of the particular from the general enactments, these were the initial difficulties of the codification. These laws were then adapted to nations, climates and customs in which the Latin discipline is enforced. In addition new legislation was introduced as a complement to the old which was retained in the Code. Lastly, and this makes the feat more monumental, the legislation was molded into the form of modern civil codes.

Never before in the history of Canon Law was there such a general abrogation. Compilations were abolished by Gregory the IX, collections were annulled by Boniface VIII, but never was there such wholesale abrogation. Today the Codex is the *"unicus fons"* of ecclesiastical legislation.[2] True, there are some few exceptions to this statement. The Oriental Church has a unique discipline. Substantially its legislation is untouched by the Code.[3] Liturgical laws retain their former status unless they are expressly corrected in the Code.[4] Con-

1 Wernz, op. cit., p. 383.
2 A. A. S., Vol. IX (1917), p. 439.
3 Canon 1.
4 Canon 2.

cordats are unmolested by the new legislation.[5] Indults and privileges which emanated from the Holy See remain intact unless the Code expressly revokes them.[6]

In the future canonists will not be vexed with many codices of law. The Commission for the Interpretation of the Code will insert new laws and legislative changes into the Code when occasion exacts them. This may be done only at the behest of the Roman Pontiff.[7] In recording editions to the Code the number of the Canon and paragraph will be explicitly stated.

The Code of 1918 is without doubt new legislation. Some jurists are loath to use the term, perhaps fearful of burying the "*Corpus Juris Canonici*" without honor. It is new legislation not in the sense that the basic tenets of the Church have been changed, not in the sense that the aim and end of the society have been diverted—these are ever changeless. Qualifying and modifying old laws implies a change. Objectively every transition has two terms: the "*terminus a quo*" and the "*terminus ad quem.*" The latter is usually called the new. New laws have been introduced. The external technique is an innovation in ecclesiastical discipline. The vast power of exclusion is a novelty in the juridical science. These are indications which justify the statement that the Code is new legislation.

In its skeleton-outline the Code resembles the "*Corpus Juris Canonici.*" First in order is the Bull of Promulgation. This is followed by the official establishment of the Commission for the Interpretation of the Code. Then comes the historic profession of faith originally arranged by Pius IV and later revised by the Vatican Council. Gasparri, in his unofficial index, does not consider these as part of the Code. Then comes the dispositive part of the new legislation, the "*Codex Juris Canonici.*" Though there is some similarity, there is also a notable departure

---

5 Canon 3.

6 Canon 4.

7 "*Cum Juris Canonici,*" Codex Juris Canonici, p. XL, seq.

from the order of the Decretals. The postulates of the Vatican Fathers favored no specific division. There was, however, a general tendency to favor the "*Corpus Juris Canonici.*" Their sole object was a revision of the "*Corpus Juris Canonici.*" At the outset in 1904 the program divided the work into five books in addition to a general introduction. The preliminary part of the Code consisted of "*De Summa Trinitate et Fide Catholica, De Constitutionibus, De Consuetudine, De Rescriptis.*" The Code proper was divided in the following manner: "*De Personis, De Sacramentis, De Rebus et Locis Sacris, De Delictis et Poenis, De Iudiciis.*"[8] This conspectus was offered with the proviso that necessary changes be made in the progress of the work. Finally this rough outline merged into the present form of the Code.

Modern laws are commonly divided into the administrative and the constitutive. This generic division is absent in the Code.[9] Some say the code follows the old classic division as found in the Institutes of Gaius; namely, persons, things and actions. Others claim the Code imitates the Institutions of Lancelotti which were divided into personae, res, judices and crimina.[10] Some others suggest that the order of the Code is a replica of the works which were common in Rome at the time.[11]

The Code as the Decretals comprises five books. Authors commonly called the first book of the Decretals "*Index.*" In reality it dealt with persons in general. The "*Normae Generales*" constitute the first book of the Code. Therein the legislator proclaims the status of particular and general law as also the nature of ecclesiastical legislation. The "*Normae*" of the Decretals were gleaned from various parts of the five books, e. g., the legislation on privileges with very few titles is found in Book V, whilst rescripts are embodied in the first book.

The second book of the Decretals treats of judgments

8 A. S. S., Vol. XXXVII, p. 130.
9 Bernereggi, op. cit., p. 113.
10 Augustine, op. cit., p. 63.
11 *Archiv für Katholisches Kirchenrecht*, 1918, p. 74.

which corresponds to the fourth book of the code. Persons, moral and physical, are treated in the second book of the Code. Herein are included the hierarchy of order and jurisdiction, seculars, religious, laics living in common and confraternities.

Clerics, benefices, ecclesiastical government are arranged in the third book of the Decretals, whilst *"De Rebus"* is its counterpart in the Code. The sacraments, the sacred places and times, the divine cult, the magesterium of the Church, the benefices, and the temporalities of the Church are all included in the third book of the new law. The nearest approach to this classification in the Decretals is the fourth book which deals with *"connubium."* The other sacraments have no specific placement in the *"Corpus Juris Canonici."*

Matrimony is found in the fourth book of the Decretals; whilst *"De Processibus"* is its counterpart in the Code. The term *"De Processibus"* has been selected in preference to *"De Judiciis" "De Processibus"* is more embracing in its scope. The term is, therefore, the more appropriate; for there are many prescriptions on ecclesiastical questions and affairs which must be adjudicated and expedited judicially and extra-judicially. Negotiations which are extra-judicial are treated in the third part of the same book.[12] The process of canonization and beatification was not found in the Decretals. The first evidence of this canonical tract is detected in the works of Urban VIII and Benedict XIV.

Causes I and III of the Decretum Gratiani and the 5th Book of the Decretals correspond to *"De Delictis et Poenis"* of the Code.

Last in the order of the Code come the constitutions of the Roman Pontiffs. These serve as an appendix to the new legislation. To some extent they are a facsimile of the *"Novellae"* of Justinian. Inasmuch as they are appendices they are a replica of the Justinian Novels. The

---

12 Noval, *Commentarium Codicis Juris Canonici, De Processibus*, p. 1.

Justinian enactments, however, were published subsequent to the Code;[13] whereas these apostolic constitutions were promulgated antecedent to the Code. The *"Regulae Juris"* of Boniface VIII resemble these constitutions inasmuch as they served as a complement to the general law. These rules, however, were juridical axioms of private authority. The form of true and universal law must be attributed to the Constitutions; for they form an integral part of the Code[14] equivalent to the old enactments related in the Canons.[15] Why the codifiers did not reduce these documents to canonical form is difficult to ascertain. All the documents[16] save the *"Predecessores Nostri"* of Leo XIII have specific mention in the body of the legislation. This constitution is used in conjunction with the *"Vacante Sede Apostolica"* of Pius X in Canon 160. It is useless to state that the narrative parts are devoid of juridical value.

The Code is divided into books. The first is divided into titles and canons with paragraphs as sub-divisions. The remaining four books have parts, sometimes sections, which are divided into titles. Many titles are not subdivided into chapters and some chapters are not subdivided into articles. Each book, with its part, section, title, chapter and article has its respective inscription. Titles usually have many Canons. The 2414 Canons are usually distributed into paragraphs and these in turn into numbers. Some are without paragraphs and numbers. These detailed systematic divisions are not found in the Decretals. A more general classification into books, chapters, and titles abounded. The Canons in the Code are not a novelty in legislation. They were employed in general and particular councils. The Canon has a preceptive form which is proper to laws. In the

---

13 Muirhead, *Historical Introduction to the Private Law of Rome*, p. 374.

14 Maroto, op. cit., p. 156.

15 Noval, *Codificationis Juris Canonici Recensio Historico—Apologetica et Cod. Piano Bene. Notitia Generalis*, p. 46.

16 Canons 160, 241, 459, § 4; 884, 904, 1125.

Code, however, the hortative and directive are not wanting.

The Code is well ordered by a clear and rational system whose parts are logically distributed and connected. There is not a medley of titles and chapters ill-ordered, but a well-defined order prevails. The form is abstract as in all modern law books. The Council of Trent successfully withheld all casuistry in its disciplinary Canons. The casuistry of the Decretals with sparse abstract rules no longer thrives in jurisprudence.[17] To realize an embracing norm adapted to all possibilities should be the ideal of the legislator. In this endeavor the codifiers succeeded admirably. True, all doubtful and hypothetical cases could not be embodied in a body of laws in which succinctness is a necessity. Minuteness must be held aloof where brevity is the keynote. This postulates the necessity of a Canon 6 with its manifold prescriptions. The external technique of the Code is consonant with the times. The system of the Decretals afforded a satisfactory presentation for Feudal times. Advance in jurisprudence urged a mutation in the external form. Modern law books with their curt and pithy enactments have been eminently helpful to the people, lawyers and the legislators. Ever has the church taken what was good and useful into ecclesiastical legislation. It would be a sad commentary on ecclesiastical legislation if there were no progress in law structure. Formerly the Church played the role of forerunner. But the Pseudo-Reformation and its baneful consequences, the French Revolution and the later dream of the World Empire, the nations alternating in persecuting the Church in the 19th century, all these factors hindered the production of constructive ecclesiastical legislation. Being ever on the offensive in these trying times the external organization and its restoration occupied the Church for many years. Eventually comes the Code of 1918. Berneregg[18] out-

---

[17] *Theologische Quartal Schrift*, 1905, p. 75.

[18] Berneregg, op. cit., p. 75.

lines the purpose of codes as the most perfect scientific systematization of laws and its best expression. The former may be termed specification, the latter codification. Ferreres has well said that the disposition of a new law book should be logical, that a reading would disclose its contents.[19] These qualities may be attributed to the present Code of Canon Law.

---

19 *Rezon y Fe,* Vol. IX, p. 368.

CHAPTER III.

THE GENERAL STRUCTURE OF CANON 6.

"Codex vigentem huc usque disciplinam plerumque retinet, licet opportunas immutationes afferat. Itaque:

1. Leges quaelibet, sive universales sive particulares, praescriptis huius Codicis oppositae, abrogantur, nisi de particularibus legibus aliud expresse caveatur;

2. Canones qui ius vetus ex integro referunt, ex veteris juris auctoritate, atque ideo ex receptis apud probatos auctores interpretationibus, sunt aestimandi;

3. Canones qui ex parte tantum cum veteri iure congruunt, qua congruunt, ex iure antiquo aestimandi sunt; qua discrepant sunt ex sua ipsorum sententia dijudicandi;

4. In dubio num aliquod canonum praescriptum cum veteri iure discrepet, a veteri iure non est recendum;

5. Quod ad poenas attinet, quarum in Codice nulla fit mentio, spirituales sint vel temporales, medicinales vel, ut vocant, vindicativae, latae vel ferendae sententiae, eae tanquam abrogatae habeantur;

6. Si qua ex ceteris disciplinaribus legibus, quae usque adhuc viguerunt, nec explicite nec implicite in Codice contineatur, ea vim omnem amisisse dicenda est, nisi in probatis liturgicis libris reperiatur, aut lex sit iuris divini sive positivi sive naturalis."

The relation of the Canons, or the Code in its internal technique, to other enactments is substantially expressed in Canon 6. The *"Providentissima Mater"* presents the Code as the officially promulgated body of ecclesiastical laws.[1] The Sacred Congregation of Seminaries and Universities labeled the Code the *"unicus fons"* of the abid-

---

[1] *Codex Juris Canonici*, Rome, 1918.

ing legislation. The legislator has constructed Canon 6 to show the relation between the Canons and preceding enactments.

Falco injudiciously criticizes the general structure of Canon 6. It begins, he avers, with a superficial observation on the contents of the code. Thence the legislator proceeds to deductions indicated by "*itaque.*" The six dispositions which follow are of an entirely different nature.[2] The introductory clause to the Canon assures the reader that much of the ancient discipline has been retained and opportune changes have been made. Prescriptions of the new law which are in substantial accord with the old are certainly retained in the Code.[3] Mutations are commonly divided into substantial and partial. Every substantial change in legislation implies abrogation. The dispositions of numbers 1, 5, 6 deal with substantial ablations. Accidental changes in juridical terminology are known as derogations. Rules of interpretation for canons which derogate quondam laws are found in number 3. Finally Canon 6, n. 4, prescribes norms for Canons in which there is doubt of a discrepancy. To challenge the logic of the structure of Canon 6 is ridiculous. Each number contains either a principle of mutation or retention. The dispositions introduced by "*itaque*" are not inconsequential.

The Canon contains all the possible forms of relation to the "*vetus ius.*" The prescriptions of the Code according to the norms of Canon 6 are the determining factors in the relation. Thus Canon 6, n. 1, presents opposition as a determinant of abrogation. Number 2 has the determinant of retention of the old law, whilst partial retention is emphasized in number 3. The doubtful discrepancy between laws ever favors the former enactment.[4] Omission, as a final determinant of abrogation, is realized in numbers 5 and 6.

---

2 Falco, *Introduzione Allo Studio del "Codex Juris Canonici,"* p. 50.

3 Canon 6, n. 2.

4 Canon 6, n. 4.

CHAPTER IV.

ABROGATION.

The principle of abrogation is freely employed by the legislator in Canon 6. The greater part of the Canon deals with this principle. Recall of legislation is the most common form of the cessation of law. In juridical terminology the cessation of law from extrinsic reasons is called abrogation, derogation, and obrogation. Some authors introduce surrogation into this division.[1] Surrogation, however, is the introduction of an entirely new legislative act. Whereas, here the subject under observation is the ablation of the law.

To relegate the obsolete, to annul the contradictory, to institute partial ablations these were some of the general purposes outlined by the "*Arduum Sane Munus.*" Canon 6 has admirably succeeded in fulfilling the intentions of the initial codifiers. To relegate, to annul is simply to abrogate, or to derogate a law. Abrogation is commonly defined as the total ablation of a law.[2] Whenever a law is abrogated it is destitute of juridical value and ceases to bind its subjects. Derogation is the partial revocation of a legislative enactment. "*Derogatur legi, cum pars detrahitur*" is an axiom borrowed from Roman law.[3]

Obrogation has caused not a little confusion among the jurists. It is ordinarily defined as the introduction of a contrary law.[4] The definition seems inadequate. Canon

---

1 Maroto, op. cit., p. 260; Wernz, op. cit., p. 141.

2 Vermeersch-Creusen, op. cit., p. 76; Lehmkuhl, *Theologia Moralis*, Vol. I, p. 118; Wernz, loc. cit.; Suarez, *De Legibus*, l. VI, cap. 27, n. 14; Schmalzgrueber, op. cit., n. 51.

3 l. 102 D. 50, 16; Suarez, loc. cit.; Wernz, loc. cit.; Schmalzgrueber, loc. cit., *Corpus Juris Civilis*, Dig. 16, 102.

4 Vermeersch-Creusen, op. cit., p. 76.

22 which is a partial restatement of Canon 6 gives a more exact definition. At a first reading of the Canon it is noticeable that it implies more than the mere introduction of a contrary law. Obrogation takes place according to Canon 22 in different ways.

"Lex posterior, a competente auctoritate lata, obrogat priori, si id expresse edicat, aut sit illi directe contraria, aut totam de integro ordinet legis prioris materiam;" . . . . Canon. 22.

The express repeal of a law, direct contrariety, and total rearrangement of matter are three forms of obrogation recognized by the legislator. It may, therefore, be realized without presupposing a contrary law. Just as abrogation and derogation may be used without involving a contrary law, so too obrogation. An instance may be alleged. The legislator discovers a law unsuitable to the conditions of the times. The enactment may be totally rejected or may be transformed as to become conformable to the circumstances. Still there need not be contradictory matter. The Roman jurists defined abrogation "*Mutare aliquid ex prima lege.*"[5] The keynote of the definition is changed. The forms of this mutation is quoted above in Canon 22. Obrogation, therefore, may be defined as the introduction of a change in legislation. The mutation may be partial or total as it expresses an antipode to derogation or abrogation respectively. Obrogation, therefore, will indicate the new law which has changed the old, whilst abrogation and derogation will merely point out the ablation of the old law. Take note of an example to illustrate the point. The impediment of affinity in the old law extended to the third degree. Today the second degree is the boundary line of the impediment. The latter obrogated the former; whilst the former has been derogated.

The principles of abrogation, derogation and obrogation are formulated by the competent legislator. The

---

5 Ulpian, 1, 3.

"imperium" of the Catholic Church, as of every society, postulates the necessity of a legislator. The legislative power not only enacts new laws but also changes and abolishes laws no longer fulfilling their end. The *"imperium"* of the Church has for its object the external discipline of the Church. The external worship, the sacred rites, the administration of the sacraments, the canonical election and institutions of its ministers, fasts, feasts, religious orders, the administration of the temporal affairs of the Church, these, in fine, constitute the matter of ecclesiastical legislation. These canonical matters must be protected in their integrity. The members of the Church must ever retain the inviolate right to use them. That the principles underlying these institutions be safeguarded, that unity or at least uniformity be observed in their use, that the mark of Catholicity be not thwarted—for these reasons Christ instituted the Church endowed with a unique legislative power.

The pope, as the successor of St. Peter, is the appointed protector of the moral bond which exists between the Church and its members. This supreme office is called primacy of jurisdiction. Such a post in any society is the first, the supreme power of ruling and governing said society to its end and purpose.[6] The power of the primacy is not limited to matters pertaining to faith and morals, but also is extended to ordinary discipline.[7] That the votaries of that society be "not as little children tossed to and fro" by uncertainty or doubt in matters of discipline the note of infallibility has been tendered to the primate, the supreme ruler. The Church is infallible in its discipline as a secondary object of infallibility. This is understood not in the sense that her laws are immutable nor in the sense that the present laws are the most opportune and most useful but it implies that nothing in the discipline of the Church can be found which is contrary to faith or morals, or which could converge unto

6 Bouix, *Tractatus De Papa,* Tom. I, p. 231.

7 Hermann, *Institutiones Theologiae Dogmaticae,* Vol. I, p. 367.

the detriment of the Church and the loss of souls. The mission of the Church is to keep the faith in its integrity and to lead the people to salvation by teaching them to observe all things which Christ commands. The discipline could not therefore prescribe or enjoin or tolerate anything contrary to faith and morals or create a hazard for souls.[8]

Boniface the VIII improvised an axiom which has echoed and re-echoed thruout the centuries. It expresses in its amplitude the legislative power of the Roman Pontiff. He acclaims "*Romanus pontifex iura omnia in scrinio pectoris sui censetur habere.*"[9] Dr. Gillmann[10] avers that Boniface the VIII did not ascribe to the pontiff universal legislative power nor was he acclaimed a plenipotentiary. On the contrary, he declares the context reveals merely the distinction between the universal and the particular law. The context from which the phrase above was snatched reads thus:

> *Licet Romanus Pontifex, qui iura omnia in scrinio pectoris sui censetur habere, constitutionem condendo posteriorem priorem, quamvis de ipsa mentionem non faciat, revocare noscatur: quia tamen locorum specialium et personarum singularium consuetudines et statuta, quum sint facti et in facto consistant, potest probabiliter ignorare: ipsis, dum tamen sint rationabilia, per constitutionem a se noviter editam, nisi expresse caveatur in ipsa, non intelligitur in aliquo derogare.*

"*Iura omnia*" is the center of the disputed point. The universal and not the particular law is encased in his bosom. True, particular law is immune from the general principle of abrogation recorded in this quotation. But it seems Boniface presupposes the plenipotentiary power in this statement. The pontiff merely limits the exercise of the power in favor of particular legislation. Benedict XIV, the great canonist, manifests the purpose of and the unlimited powers of the sovereign pontiff in this behalf. The legislative power is in existence not only

---

8 Hermann, op. cit., p. 314; *Council of Trent,* Sess. XXII, Can. 7; Pius VI in Constitutio "*Auctorem Fidei.*"

9 C. 1. in VI°, De Const. 1. 2.

10 *Archiv für Katholisches Kirchenrecht,* 1926, p. 156.

to direct through counsel and admonitions, but also to command through laws, punishing also the unrighteous with salubrious penalties and coercing the contumacious.[11]

The power to enact laws implies the competency to abrogate. The latter is one function of the legislative authority. Some juridical aphorisms forcibly portray this thought: "*Res omnis per quascumque causas nascitur, per easdem dissolvi potest; Qui legem tulit, legem abrogat.*" Schmalzgrueber asks the question, who can abrogate? His response is "*Qui eam tulit, quia haec dependet a voluntate ejusdem.*"[12] To abrogate a law does not require the same physical person who enacted it. This power, needless to say, is not vested in one pontiff alone. It resides in all who have the primacy of jurisdiction. The legitimate successor is competent to abrogate the laws of the predecessor. In no wise can any pontiff curtail the power of his successor. Papal constitutions sometimes contain the clause "*hac immutabili et in perpetuum valitura constitutione.*"[13] Such a clause is not destined to invalidate subsequent acts of the successor[14] nor does it tend to curtail his power; for, "*par in parem non habet imperium.*"[15] The legislator attaches an especial juridical sanction to laws which have such a clause appended. Pirhing[16] advances the theory that the laws of general councils are not abolished unless a derogatory clause is annexed to the posterior enactment, as, "*non obstante quacumque lege aut constitutione in Concilio generali edita.*" But if the dispositions of the law, he continues, require no such derogatory clause, a general derogatory clause suffices to postulate an ablation. Noval[17] refutes assertions which attempt to canonize the laws of the Council of

---

11 Benedict XIV, "*Ad Assiduas,*" Vol. III, pars. 2, p. 225.
12 Schmalzgrueber, op. cit., p. 220, n. 53.
13 Augustine, op. cit., p. 103; Reiffenstuel, op. cit., Book I, p. 118.
14 Suarez, op. cit., cap. XXVI, p. 445, n. 1.
15 C. 20, in VI°, I, 6.
16 Pirhing, *Ius Canonicum,* Vol. I, p. 53.
17 Noval, op. cit., p. 47, seq.

Trent. An especial predilection is manifested for this Council because of its solemn and invaluable sessions. The codifiers are accused of conserving its enactments as subsidiary sources for interpreting and supplying vacancies in legislation. Nothing can be detected in the Code which would warrant such a privilege to the laws of Trent. One Canon 6 deals with the subsidiary sources of the Code. The old law in general is esteemed as such an interpretative aid. The words *"ius vetus"*, *"veteris juris"*, *"a vetere iure"*, *"a iure antiquo"*, *"legibus quae hucusque viguerunt"* shows no preference to the Tridentine laws. Again if a prior law is bound up by an oath (*"non juramento assertorio de praesenti sed promissorio de futuro"*) which reads into it immunity from abrogation the law is not countermanded unless express mention is made to that effect.[18] The reasons for this assertion is that the legislator is mindful of a law which has an oath attached and hence abrogation would be invalid. As stated above, the predecessor cannot curtail the power of the successor. Furthermore, no allowance is made for such enactments in Canon 6.

What is necessary and valid matter for abrogation? To annul an existing enactment justly and licitly it must be effected *"propter bonum commune."*[19] There must ever be a just cause for a licit ablation. An illicit annulment never affects the validity. It is ever valid; for the obligation of the law depends on the will of the legislator. The action may be illicit because the abrogation of a useful law is the abuse of power and jurisdiction. The primacy is entrusted to him to rule subjects through just laws.[20] An unjust or useless law is not the only matter suited for abrogation. To make a licit annulment it is sufficient that the law is too rigorous, or less useful than another, or that a greater benefit is hoped from its recall, or that

18 Leurenio, *Jus Canonicum Universum*, Vol. I, p. 110.

19 St. Thomas, *Summa Theologica*, Prima Secundae, q. 97, art. 1; Suarez, op. cit., cap. 25, n. 3.

20 Schmalzgrueber, op. cit., p. 220.

greater dangers and evils are in some way avoided. The just law may be omitted or changed for a law more just.[21] Whatever be the nature of the law emanating from the sovereign pontiff, it obligates the subjects of the Church at all times. Whatever the motivating cause of the legislation may be, whatever impending danger is gripping the Church due to a law, whatever may be the utility of a peculiar enactment, subjects are bound in conscience to observe it. Liceity concerns the consciences of the legislators. A doubt concerning a valid abrogation has no significance; for the law ever retains its binding force.

A last requisite for abrogation of law is the publication of the act. There are two recognized ways of declaring null and void any legislation: 1) the withdrawal of the obligations without imposing another onus; 2) the revocation of one obligation which is supplanted by another.[22] Both forms are used in Canon 6. Numbers 5 and 6 of this Canon advocate the first class; whilst the second class is sponsored by numbers 1, 3 and 4. Canon 6 embodies the principles of abrogation relative to the old law. Henceforth, the official bulletin of the "*Acta Apostolicae Sedis,*" will pronounce the declarations of nullity. The task at hand, the abrogation of the old laws, has its determinants in Canon 6.

---

21 Suarez, op. cit., cap XXV, p. 444, n. 6.
22 Suarez, op. cit., cap. XXVII, p. 450, n. 2.

CHAPTER V.

OPPOSITION OF LAWS A DETERMINANT OF ABROGATION.

Canon 6, n. 1:

"Leges quaelibet, sive universales sive particulares, praescriptis huius Codicis oppositae, abrogantur, nisi de particularibus legibus aliud expresse caveatur."

In the *"Schema"* of 1912 Canon 6 was not extant. When the codifiers finished their huge task there was need of principles to govern the interrelation of both laws, the old and the new. The legislator, conversant with the history of Canon law, realized the utter uselessness of promulgating a Code without establishing certain principles of abrogation, derogation, and retention relative to preceding legislation. Without a flaw these have been posited in Canon 6.

Opposition as evinced in Canon 6, n. 1 is a determinant of abrogation. It may be defined as the relation of two laws identical in matter and different in form. The absence of identity in matter is not opposition but disparity. Laws opposed one to another postulate the suspension of one obligation and the introduction of the opposite. This opposition may be negative, or as commonly called contradictory. To command or allow an action now which formerly was prohibited is a quasi-contradictory prescription.[1] Formal contradiction is the introduction of an enactment which is the negation of an erstwhile affirmation.[2] This is in need of no interpretation. An example of a contradictory law is Canon 1251, § 2, which allows the use of meat and fish at the same collation.

1 Suarez, op. cit., p. 450, n. 2, cap. XXVII.
2 Suarez, loc. cit.

This is contradictory to the law of Benedict XIV which prohibited the use of meat and fish at the same meal.

There seems to be another form of opposition, called contrariety:

"Regulae et particulares constitutiones singularum religionum, canonibus huius Codicis non contrariae vim suam servant; quae vero eisdem opponuntur, abrogatae sunt." Canon 489.

Opposition and contrariety are considered on a parity by the legislator. Whatever is not contrary retains its juridical value; but whatever is opposed is abrogated. Opposition is a more generic term than contrariety. Suarez[3] defines contrariety as a positive repugnance which exists between two laws. It usually occurs in affirmative laws which command repugnant acts. Ordinarily both laws are affirmative. One, however, may be negative. In case of the latter it may not be immediately and formally opposed; for then there would be contradiction. In a decision of the Sacra Romana Rota contrariety is used synonomously with incompatibility.[4]

Vermeersch offers a nominal definition of contrariety.[5] That a valid abrogation be assured the contrariety must be certain and invincible. This statement is irrefutable. He continues, direct contrariety is immediate contrariety. This is exemplified in Canon 1251, § 2, which is in direct opposition to the law of Benedict XIV. As stated above, this is contradiction not contrariety. Vermeersch explains further that indirect contrariety is oblique contrariety. This occurs when the legislator enacts a positive law which does not wholly coincide with the former law or becomes an exception to the general law. He then concludes that not all the juridical force of the first law is lost but both may subsist at the same time. This form of relation between the former legislation and the Code has especial provision in Canon 6, n. 3. The question in

3 Suarez, loc. cit.

4 A. A. S., Vol. V (1913), p. 223, seq.

5 Vermeersch-Creusen, op. cit., Vol. I, p. 76.

Canon 6, n. 1 deals not with derogation or partial contrariety in laws but treats substantial contrariety or abrogation. An exception to the law is usually termed a dispensation or a privilege. The legislator has also provided a special treatise for this juridical element in the Code.

Blat[6] adds little to the concept of contrariety. Laws directly contrary to pre-existing enactments abrogate them; for both cannot exist at the same time. This can never happen when the following principle is applicable: "*expedit concordare iura iuribus et earum correctiones 'si sustinere valeant' evitare.*" This rule is usually applied to Canon 6, n. 4 and not to contrariety.

Barbosa advances the notion of contrariety by citing a few examples. Contrariety comes from the proposition of contraries. Legitimate and illegitimate, present and absent are contrary terms.[7]

The most adequate concept of contrariety is taken from Suarez in the aforementioned quotation. It is positive repugnance or incompatibility between two laws. The canonist must determine the repugnance and the incompatibility of each individual law in applying the principles of interpretation.

There are also degrees of contrariety. Enactments may be substantially or partially repugnant. Substantial incompatibility belongs exclusively to number 1 of Canon 6. It entails the unlimited ablation of the former law. Whenever the basic elements of a law are contrary a substantial contrariety ensues. The impediment of affinity in the old law was based on perfect coition. Today affinity has its foundation in a "matrimonium validum sive consummatum sive ratum tantum".[8] Partial contrariety, on the other hand, is recognized by the legislator when the basic principles of a law are kept intact but the

6 Blat, *Commentarium Textus Codicis Juris Canonici,* Vol. I, p. 106.

7 Barbosa, *Tractatus Varii,* p. 38.

8 Capello, *Tractatus Canonico, Moralis De Sacramentis iuxta Codicem Juris Canonici,*Vol. III, *De Matrimonio,* p. 568.

extension or embrace of the new law is contrary to the old. The legislator has set aside a special number in Canon 6 for this form of contrariety.

Contraries cannot exist at the same time; for, they are mutually exclusive. The one law is posited, whilst the other is simultaneously removed. To have two laws which are contrary would render law and its obligations odious. It would be the equivalent of saying that a thing can exist and cannot exist at the same time. These concepts belong to the habit of first principles which never can be effaced. Laws then according to Canon 6 n. 1 which are contrary to the prescriptions of the code are abrogated.

Article I—Universal Laws.

"Leges quaelibet sive universales . . . . huius codicis oppositae . . . . abrogantur."

Universal laws opposed to the Code are abrogated. By reason of extension, laws are commonly divided into universal and particular, inasmuch as they have binding force throughout the universal Church or some part thereof; as they obligate all faithful or some class of persons they are divided into general and singular; as to application, there is a further division into common and special as they establish the ordinary rule or an exception to the same.[9] Not rarely are these terms used promiscuously. Modern authors call that law universal which has juridical force throughout Christendom.[10] The Code apparently recognizes no determined division. Particular law is not used in antithesis to universal law alone. In Canons 14 and 20 particular law is used in contrast to the general law. Peculiar law, in Canon 83, is opposed to the general. *"Jus commune"* is identified with general law in Canons 336, § 1 and 81. Civil law in Canon 1112 is termed *"ius specialise."*[11]

---

9 Lijdsman, op. cit., p. 19.

10 Maroto, op. cit., p. 35, seq.; Raus, *Institutiones Canonicae,* p. XVI; Blat, op. cit., p. 31.

11 Falco, op. cit., p. 42.

Universal laws are the enactments of the Pontiffs, the General Councils, and the Congregations of the Holy See. Legislation emanating from the General Councils and the Congregations have not the force of universal law unless they have the approbation of the Sovereign Pontiff.[12] It is well to recall that universal laws as they existed in the old regime are here considered. The abrogation is directed primarily to the laws surviving the principles of abrogation in the old law.

To make the study of the old legislation more accurate and more facile it is necessary to indicate the external character of these universal laws. In the Middle Ages the pontifical acts were divided into two classes: 1) "*Decreta et Decretales,*" 2) "*Constitutiones et Rescripta*". At the time of Gratian "*Decretum*" and "*Decretales*" were used promiscuously. They were generic terms which determined all papal enactments. Later a distinction was introduced between these two terms. "*Decreta*" were pontifical acts emanating spontaneously from the Holy See. Whilst "*Decretales*" were of the same species of legislation but they were promulgated on the request of some one. "*Constitutio*" at the time of Gratian was defined as a law enacted by the Roman Pontiff.[13] Gratian calls it "*lex est constitutio scripta.*"[14] On the other hand "*Rescriptum*" was a response given by the Roman Pontiff for a particular case. The "*Decretum*" is therefore identified with the "*Constitutio;*" whilst a similarity abounded between the "*Rescriptum*" and the "*Decretales.*" Constitutions and Decretals are later used in antithesis. This fact is revealed in a gloss on the "*Rex Pacificus*": "*Constitutio est quam princeps facit proprio motu; Decretalis epistola quando respondet ad consulationem.*"[15] Nearer to our time the word "*Constitutio*" is used for all papal enactments. In a very limited sense, however, papal constitutions have four characteristics:

---

12 Wernz, op. cit., p. 109.
13 Maroto, op. cit., p. 392.
14 C. 3, D. 1.
15 Maroto, op. cit., p. 393.

1) they come immediately from the Roman Pontiff, 2) they are presented "*motu proprio*", 3) the solemn form of a Bull is attached to them, 4) they deal with matters of greater importance. An instance of this type is found in the "*Providentissima Mater Ecclesiae*" which officially promulgated the Code.[16]

The "*motu proprio*" as the word indicates is not edited at the request of another person, but proceeds spontaneously from the Roman Pontiff. Generally the "*motu proprio*" is not a legislative enactment. In some instances, however, the contrary has been observed; e. g., the "*Sacrorum Antistitum*" of September 1, 1910.[17] Its subject-matter is less grave than that of the Constitutions and it is usually confined to administrative negotiations. These were once called "*Decreta.*" Today "*Decreta*" are the acts of the Roman Congregations.

"*Litterae Apostolicae*" are acts of the Roman Pontiff presented in the form of a solemn letter thru Bulls or Briefs. In form they resemble the constitutions; in matter the "*motu proprio.*" If they are presented in the form of a Bull the act begins with the name of the pontiff to which is added "*Servus Servorum Dei.*"[18] These are signed by the Cardinal Chancellor and all his officials, or by the Cardinal Chancellor and the Cardinal Prefect of the Congregation to which the matter was submitted.[19] The Constitutions are signed by the Cardinal Chancellor and the Cardinal Secretary of State or the Cardinal Prefect of the competent Congregation. In the "*Brevia,*" a less solemn form of the "*Litterae Apostolicae,*" the name and number of the pontiff is noted, v. g. "*Pius Papa XI*" or "*Pius PP. XI.*" Today these are commonly signed by the Cardinal Secretary of State.[20]

"*Litterae Encylclicae*" *or* "*Epistolae Encyclicae*" or simply "*Encyclicae*" are those acts of the Pontiff which

---

16 *Codex Juris Canonici.*
17 Maroto, op. cit., p. 395.
18 Phillips, op. cit., p. 26.
19 Maroto, op. cit., p. 401.
20 Lijdsman, op. cit., p. 59.

expose to the bishops and faithful the mind of the Church on matters doctrinal or disciplinary. "*Epistolae*" or "*Litterae Pontificiae*" or "*Epistolae Pontificiae*" or "*Litterae*" are letters in which the pope proffers admonitions or instructions, or in which he expresses congratulations, benevolence and the like. The signature of the pope is attached to these unostentatious acts.[21]

"*Instructiones*" ordinarily do not contain obligatory prescriptions. They usually express doctrinal explanations, directive norms and admonitions. There have been not a few Instructions which contained veritable prescriptions.[22]

"*Chirographa*" are letters which are personally signed by the Pontiff. Sometimes these are also called "*Litterae autographae.*"[23]

"*Rescripta*" are responses made on request of a petitioner. It matters little whether they are in the form of Bulls or Briefs. There are many "*Litterae Apostolicae*" given in the form of Briefs which are mere rescripts.[24]

The General Councils of the Church also contain disciplinary enactments. They never function or legislate validity without the consent and approval of the Roman Pontiff. The dogmatic declarations in Councils are ordinarily called "*Decreta.*" The disciplinary enactments are embodied in "*Canones.*"[25] The Council of Trent is at variance with this common form. The precepts which contained the restoration of discipline are called "*Decreta de Reformatione;*" whilst matters which pertained to faith are embedded in "*Decreta.*" The solemn condemnations of erroneous propositions are called "*Canones.*" These began with "*si quis dixerit*" and terminated with "*anathema sit.*"

---

21 Lijdsman, op. cit., pp. 55, 59.
22 Maroto, op. cit., p. 397.
23 Lijdsman, op. cit., p. 59.
24 Maroto, op. cit., p. 397.
25 Phillips, op. cit., p. 29.

The legislative power conceded to some of the Congregations has never been officially retracted. The "*Decretum*" is the common juridical term for Congregational Acts. Legislative competency was acknowledged in the Congregation of the Council in 1857,[26] to the Congregation of the Propagation of the Faith in 1652,[27] in the Congregation of Rites 1846.[28] Nearer to our times the legislative authority of the Congregations has increased.[29] The "*Declarationes*" are norms of interpretation. "*Resolutiones*" are responses to particular cases. "*Decisiones*" are judicial sentences. The first is classified with universal law; the rest "*per se*" do not belong to this category.[30]

All universal laws opposed to the prescriptions of the Code are abrogated. The opposition must be certain. Wherever there is a doubtful discrepancy Canon 6 n. 4 establishes interpretative norms. The contrariety must be substantial; for, the partial opposition in laws has prescriptions elsewhere.[31] A law discarded by the principles of abrogation is relegated to the history of Canon Law, whilst other enactments may be used as subsidiary sources of the new law as it is evinced in Canon 6, n. 2, n. 3 and n. 4.

Article II—Particular Law.

"Leges quaelibet . . . . sive particulares, praescriptis huius Codicis oppositae, abrogantur, nisi de particularibus legibus aliud expresse caveatur." Canon 6, n. 1.

All positive legislation, be it divine or human, is radically a participation of the eternal law. Natural law has an immediate participation in the eternal. The positive laws have a three-fold object: to enlarge, to determine more and more, and to attach a sanction to the

26 Maroto, op. cit., p. 410.
27 *Collectanea S .Congregationis De Propaganda Fide*, Vol. 1, n. 119.
28 *Collectio Auth. S. R. C.*, n. 2916.
29 Maroto, op. cit., p. 411.
30 Maroto, loc. cit.; Wernz, op. cit., p. 109.
31 Canon 6, n. 3.

natural law.[32] A similar relation exists between the universal and the particular law. The latter enhances the scope of the general legislation, determines it more minutely, and ratifies it. The ecclesiastical legislator thruout history had made allowance for particular legislation. A Code of laws could not embody all possible contingencies which would be suitable to all climates and temperaments thruout Christendom. For this reason the Church has ever recognized particular legislation.

Particular laws may be personal or territorial.[33] Territoriality of law affects persons who are restricted to a specified area. Who are competent to enact particular laws? The Roman Pontiff, the primate of jurisdiction, certainly has the power to enact particular laws. The Roman Congregations also are qualified to institute particular laws. It has been noted above that both the Pontiff and under given conditions the Roman Congregations validly enact universal laws. *A fortiori,* then, both are empowered to legislate in the particular field.

The papal and curial enactments obligate a certain class of people, as the religious, or people living in a determined territory as the concordats. Ordinarily, these particular laws are found amassed in the sources of general law. Besides these there are other sources of particular legislation. The plenary councils, the provincial councils, the diocesan synod, the extra-synodal statutes, the prescriptions of cathedral chapters, the statutes of religious chapters and all other agencies which derive their competency from common law, are qualified to enact particular laws.

Jurists divide particular legislation into three classes: 1) *"jus contra legem,"* 2) *"jus praeter legem,"* 3) *"jus secundum legem."* The purpose of particular law is to enlarge on the scope of the general legislation.[34] Wherever the legislator has left deficiencies in common law

---

32 Hilling, *Allgemeine Normen,* p. 34.
33 Bargilliat, *Praelectiones Juris Canonici,* tom. 8, p. 5.
34 Vering, *Theologische Bibliothek,* Kirchenrecht, p. 346.

the competent superior may supply the particular law or statute. Such laws add a force and a support to the common law.[35] These are the *"ius praeter legem."* Some particular laws *"ius secundum legem,"* are so called because they are not of diverse matter. These dispose and discern the common law. Seldom do they add or detract from the general legislation. They are merely accessory to the principal.[36] The *"ius contra legem"* is a particular enactment which is adverse to the general law.[37] This disposition in particular laws is the theme of Canon 6, n. 1.

Historically particular legislation always was immune from the principles of abrogation, unless the legislator made express mention to the contrary.

> *"Licet Romanus Pontifex, qui iura omnia in scrinio pectoris sui censetur habere, constitutionem condendo posteriorem priorem, quamvis de ipsa mentionem non faciat, revocare noscatur: quia tamen locorum specialium et personarum singularium consuetudines et statuta, quum sint facti et in facto consistant, potest probabiliter ignorare: ipsis dum tamen sint rationabilia, per constitutionem a se noviter editam, nisi expresse caveatur in ipsa, non intelligitur in aliquo derogare."* [38]

The earlier constitutions did not ordinarily abrogate particular law but dealt wholly with general legislation. The reasons why particular legislation was left intact are found in the proclamation above. Particular laws are facts and remain facts, *"Cum sint facti et in facto consistant potest probabiliter ignorare"*. Since such laws are innumerable they cannot all be known by the legislator. An abrogatory clause is annexed to a particular law when the legislator expressly states it.[39] Secondly *"dum sint rationabilia .. .. .. nisi expresse caveatur in ipsa, non intelligitur in aliquo derogare,"* whilst these laws remain reasonable the legislator does not intend to abrogate them. This condition may be

---

35 Benedict XIV, *De Synodo Dioecesano,* Lib. XII, cap. XVI, 1, p. 73.
36 Pirhing, op. cit., p. 54, Lib. 1, tit. 2, Sect. III.
37 A. A. S., Vol. XVI (1924), p. 107.
38 C. 1, de constitutionibus, 1, 2 in VI°.
39 Pirhing, op. cit., p. 54.

alleged whenever said laws are known or unknown to the legislator. From the general tenor of the new common law the pontiff can gauge if any particular law would be unreasonable. Whenever the pope legislates anew it is a juridical presumption that the particular is not abrogated. Express mention of abrogation is necessary.

In Canon 6, n. 1 the legislator expressly mentions the abrogation of contrary particular laws. The nature of contrariety as explained under general legislation is also applied here. In some dioceses there was a statute prohibiting the transfer of mass stipends to extra-diocesan priests without the permission of the ordinary. The statute was challenged on the score of Canon 838, which reads:

"Qui habent Missarum numerum de quibus sibi liceat libere disponere, possunt eas tribuere sacerdotibus sibi acceptis, dummodo probe sibi constet eos esse omni exceptione maiores vel testimonio proprii Ordinarii commendatos."

A resolution of the Congregation of the Council upheld the contention of the challenger.[40] Kinane [41] makes a deduction from this decision. Facultative laws in the Code, introduced by the words "*possunt*," "*queunt*," etc., abolish all laws, whether general or particular, which in any way restrict the power or the permission conceded by them. There was an inclination, he continues. in many quarters to regard particular dispositions of this kind rather "*praeter legem*" than "*contra legem.*" All forms of law, therefore, are abrogated by Canon 6, n. 1.

"*Nisi de legibus particularibus aliud expresse caveatur*" is the exceptive clause in the Canon 6, n. 1. Concordats retain the juridical value attached to them at the promulgation of the Code. Canon 3 expressly declares that these pacts are unassailable:

---

40 A. A. S., Vol. XIII (1921), p. 228, seq.

41 *Irish Ecclesiastical Record,* 1921, p. 423, seq.

"Codicis canones initas ab Apostolica Sede cum variis Nationibus conventiones nullatenus abrogant aut iis aliquid obrogant; eae idcirco perinde ac in praesens vigere pergent, contrariis huius Codicis praescriptis minime obstantibus."

The Oriental discipline[42] in an extended sense is particular legislation. The Code primarily affects the Latin Church. It obligates the Orientals only in certain circumstances: 1) when the Canon expressly states a prescription for the Orientals;[43] 2) when a Canon implicitly involves the Orientals;[44] 3) when doctrinal matters are embodied in Canons.[45] Prescriptions of the Oriental Church which are contrary to the Canons are certainly abrogated. The opposition to the Canons determines the ablation. It seems, therefore, that Oriental legislation contrary to legislation affecting the Orientals is null and void. Hence, it would not be amiss to conclude that Canon 6, n. 1 determines the abrogation of some Oriental legislation.

Other particular laws marked with an evident contrariety are abrogated unless express mention is made to the opposite. In some Canons there are phrases with such qualifications; namely, "*firma contraria lege fundationis,*"[46] "*nisi aliter in casibus particularibus a Sancta Sede provisum,*" [47] "*dummodo statuta ecclesiae propriae non requirant,*" [48] "*nisi obstant ecclesiae statuta,*" [49] "*salvis peculiaribus constitutionibus,*" [50] "*nisi aliud iure*

---

42 "*Licet in Codice iuris canonici Ecclesiae quoque Orientalis disciplina saepe referatur, ipse tamen unam respicit Latinam Ecclesiam, neque Orientalem obligat, nisi di iis agatur, quae ex ipsa rei natura etiam Orientalem afficiunt.*" Canon 1.

43 Canons 98, 257, 366, § 2; 1097, etc.

44 A declaration of the divine law, v.g., receiving Viaticum in danger of death.

45 Maroto, op. cit., p. 165.

46 Canon 403.

47 Canon 235.

48 Canon 418, § 1.

49 Canon 422, § 2.

50 Canon 162.

caveatur."[51] Canons which have these clauses appended are veritable exceptions to the general character of Canon 6, n. 1.

In the abrogation of particular laws no other exceptions are tolerated. It is of no avail if laws emanate "*motu proprio*" from the Holy See, if the decrees of the congregations are confirmed "*in forma communi*" or "*in forma specifica*" or if the same confirmation is attached to plenary or provincial councils—all are abolished when there is a conflict in the laws. The Decrees of a particular Council, as Baltimore, are confirmed "*in forma specifica.*" This does not assimilate or absorb its enactments into the common law. They ever remain the same. Should these become part of the universal laws then the exceptive clause in Canon 6, n. 1 would have no utility for Baltimore.

The old juridical axiom, "*generi per speciem derogatur,*" is not serviceable in Canon 6. The general law is derogated by the special. Some[52] interpreted this "*Regula Juris*" with this connotation: the special law derogates the general, be it antecedent or subsequent to the common law. Leurenio[53] gives a reason for this limitation of law. Abrogation should be avoided as much as possible. There can never be abrogation when a contrariety exists between a prior general law and a posterior special enactment. There cannot be adequate contrariety, therefore, it is only derogation.[54] All authors agree that there would be a limitation of the general law. If such jurisprudence were interpreted as affecting the personality or the territoriality of the law, it would have no juridical value today. Canon 6, n. 1 abolishes all contrary laws. Leurenio[55] and Icard[56] presuppose that the

51 Canon 172.

52 Leurenio, op. cit., p. 110; Wernz, p. 141; Zallinger, *Institutiones Juris Ecclesiasticae,* lib. 1, tit. 2, p. 134; Schmalzgrueber, op. cit., p. 220, n. 52; Reiffenstuel, op. cit., n. 496, p. 119; Suarez, op. cit., p. 452, n. 13.

53 Leurenio, loc. cit.

54 Suarez, loc. cit.

55 Leurenio, loc. cit.

56 Icard, *Praelectiones Juris Canonici,* p. 65.

axiom deals exclusively with common law. It is merely the question of the *"genus"* and *"species"* of any law. General laws on testaments, they continue, does not include the testaments for pious causes. The special law on pious causes does not suspend the general law on testaments, but the latter is distinguished and limited thereby. Nor would this interpretation rejuvenate the aphorism *"generi per speciem derogatur."* If a species of law is contrary to the genus it is abrogated by Canon 6, n. 1; if it is omitted it is abrogated by Canon 6, n. 6. Therefore, the axiom mentioned above is destitute of juridical value.

CHAPTER VI.

OMISSION, A DETERMINANT OF ABROGATION.

Opposition, as a determinant of abrogation, is very serviceable in attaining the purpose of the codification. The new code is now the "*unicus fons*" of ecclesiastical legislation. Contrary laws, as seen above, cannot exist and obligate subjects at the same time. Whatever would defeat the purpose of laws contained in the Code must be relegated to the history of Canon Law. On the other hand omission, another determinant of abrogation, is more extensive in its scope. Not only the laws which are opposed to the new body of laws, but also enactments which are not mentioned in the Code, are abrogated. In the past there never was a "*unicus fons*" of ecclesiastical laws. The term "*resecatis superfluis*" in the "*Rex Pacificus*" is expressive of the omission as a principle of abrogation in the time of the Decretals. Likewise, the "*Sacrosanctae Romanae Ecclesiae*" uses an equivalent term "*pluribus exipsis penitus resecatis.*" These are the only two instances in which the determinant, omission, could have been employed; for these collections are the only attempts at abrogating any other legislation. Consonant with the prescriptions of the "*Arduum sane munus*" the Code discards the obsolete and the abrogated. The omission of antecedent laws is an unassailable argument for their abrogation. Two numbers of Canon 6 have been devoted to omission as a principle of abrogation. Canon 6, n. 5 annuls all penal laws not mentioned in the Code. All other disciplinary laws which are not explicitly nor implicitly contained in the Code are abrogated.[1]

---

1 Canon 6, n. 6.

Article I—Penal Legislation.

"Quod ad poenas attinet, quarum in Codice nulla fit mentio, spirituales sint vel temporales, medicinales vel, uti vocant, vindicativae, latae vel ferendae sententiae, eae tanquam abrogatae habeantur." Canon 6, n. 5.

Penal legislation is not considered here with the usual connotation found in civil legislation. Ordinarily it implies a statute which does not obligate in conscience. There is not a moral obligation attached to this form of legislation. The object is to punish individuals for transgressions which have no moral turpitude. Penal legislation, in the canonical and moral sense, is called *"lex mixta."*[2] By reason of obligation law is divided into two classes: the moral or preceptive and the purely penal laws. The *"lex mixta"* is a composite of both forms of legislation. Wherefore, the pertinent juridical adage is frequently quoted *"nullum crimen, nulla poena sine lege."*

Canon 6, n. 5 restricts its prescriptions to penalties.[3] The phrase *"Quod ad poenas attinet"* seems to exclude all the accessories of penalties. This exclusion may not be urged too much. An essential part of penalties is the crime or the violation of the law.[4] Equally important are imputability of crime and the causes aggravating or diminishing this imputability.[5] It seems the entire fifth book follows the prescription of Canon 6, n. 5. All accessories follow their principal; therefore, all legislation which is an integral part of penalties is governed by Canon 6, n. 5. Even if these accessories of penalties did not come under the rules of Canon 6, n. 5, the other numbers of Canon 6 would give them the same juridical status. Penalties are not exclusively confined to the fifth book, but there are many penal enactments in other parts of the Code.[6] These, too, come under consideration here.

---

2 Noldin, *De Principiis Theologiae Moralis*, p. 132.
3 Cicognani, op. cit., p. 44.
4 *Codex Juris Canonici*, Liber Quintus, Pars Prima, Titulus I.
5 *Codex Juris Canonici*, Liber Quintus, Pars Prima, Titulus II.
6 Canons 132, 359, § 2; 727, 1554, 1625, 1755, § 3, etc.

What are the erstwhile sources of penal legislation? In general, they are contained in the sources of universal legislation. In the past there had been some attempts to reconstruct and detail more accurately penal enactments. Among these were the conclusions of the Councils of Constance, Basle and Trent, and the Apostolic Constitutions, especially those of Benedict XIV and Pius IX. The famous Bull "*Coena Domini*" ever remained a prominent source of censures reserved to the Holy See. This Bull was read formally at Rome on Holy Thursday. Reconstructed annually from the years 1362 to 1774 the document caused not a little trouble to commentators.[7] Some states subjected the publication of the Bull to the "*regium placet.*" Whenever the prescriptions were distasteful to the civil ruler its enforcement was violently opposed. The epoch-making period in penal legislation came October 12, 1869. On that day the "*Apostolicae Sedis*" of Pius IX was officially promulgated. At the instigation of the Vatican Postulates the new penal laws were collected and reconstructed. The "*Apostolicae Sedis*" was a syllabus of censures which supplanted the "*censurae latae sententiae*" found in the "*Corpus Juris Canonici,*" in the Council of Trent, and in the Apostolic Constitutions.[8] The Constitution did not alter the "*censurae ferendae sententiae.*" There were three classes of censures which were not abrogated by omission: 1) the censures incurred for crimes committed in the elections of the Roman Pontiff, 2) the censures regarding the internal government of Orders and Institutes of Regulars, Colleges, Congregations and other Pious Associations, 3) the censures directly instituted by the Council of Trent with the exception of the legislation on the edition of sacred books.[9] The "*poenae vindicativae latae sententiae*" remained intact.[10]

---

7 Cerato, *Censurae Vigentes*, p. 54.

8 Eichman, *Das Strafrecht des Codex Juris Canonici*, p. 20.

9 Leech, *The Constitution "Apostolicae Sedis" and the "Codex Juris Canonici,"* p. 12.

10 Eichman, op. cit., p. 20.

In these sources enumerated it is easy to apply the principles of abrogation. Any penalties not mentioned in the Code are abrogated. Particular laws are not included in this principle. Canon 6 n. 1 is not dealing with every possible discipline but merely with the common law, the complexus of laws given and promulgated by the Apostolic See for ruling the universal church.[11] A particular penal law which is contrary to the prescriptions of the fifth book is abrogated by Canon 6, n. 1.

A very complicated subject appears in connection with particular legislation. May a particular law *"praeter jus"* retain its original value when its subject-matter has been wholly rearranged by the new common law? Does the excommunication of the third Baltimore Council still obtain? Or is it absorbed and abolished by Canon 2319? The Council of Baltimore excommunicates Catholics who attempt marriage before a non-Catholic minister; the common law requires a double ceremony for excommunication, namely, that before or after the Catholic ceremony the non-Catholic minister is asked to witness the marriage.

Woywod once claimed that this particular law of Baltimore[12] is absorbed by the common law.[13] Later Woywod says "The law of the Code has superseded the particular law of the Council of Baltimore, insofar as the marriage of a Catholic with a non-Catholic before a non-Catholic minister is concerned. But the law of that Council remains, we believe, with reference to the marriage or rather attempted marriage of two Catholics before a non-Catholic minister, for the Code does not punish this offense of two Catholics with a *latae sententiae* censure (cfr. Canon 2316)."[14] Woywod adduces no arguments for the two statements. The last quotation seems to be very improbable. For Catholics incur the censure

11 Leech, op. cit., p. 11.

12 *Acta Concilii Plenarii Baltimorensis,* III, n. 127.

13 Homiletic Review, 1924, p. 848.

14 Woywod, A Practical Commentary on the Code of Canon Law, Vol. II, p. 472.

of Canon 2319 whether the attempted marriage be between two Catholics or between a Catholic and a non-Catholic. Canon 2319 reads:

"Subsunt excommunicationi latae sententiae Ordinario reservatae catholici:

"1. Qui matrimonium ineunt coram ministro acatholico contra praescriptum. Can. 1063, § 1;"

The prescriptions of Canon 1063, § 1, do not exclude an attempted marriage between two Catholics. Canon 1063, § 1, merely determines the law which must be violated to incur the censure of Canon 2319. Therefore, a Catholic attempting marriage before a non-Catholic minister with another Catholic or with a non-Catholic incurs the penalty of excommunication *"latae sententiae."*

Leech argues: "if we look upon the general law (Canon 2319, § 1) and the particular law (Baltimore) as contemplating different *"delicta"* we must conclude that the Baltimore censure is still in force (Canon 6, n. 1. And even if the Code contemplates the same case as the law of Baltimore, namely, the giving or renewal of matrimonial consent before a non-Catholic minister acting as such, yet it does not readily appear that the Baltimore censure is abrogated. For, the laws of the Baltimore Council, being particular laws, remain in force in so far, as they are not opposed to the Code."[15]

The solution of this question is of utmost importance for priests in the United States. If both censures are incurred there would be two excommunications for the same crime. A cumulus of similar penalties would seem useless where removal of contumacy is the only condition for absolution. If one censure is inflicted for a single ceremony the Baltimore prescription prevails, according to the authors quoted above. The Council of Baltimore also penalized with excommunication any attempt at mar-

---

15 Leech, op. cit., p. 92.

riage after obtaining a civil divorce. Leech claims that this penalty is still in vogue.[16]

It seems Canon 22 may be quoted to hasten a solution of the question.[17] Wherever there is a total re-arrangement of the old legislation, the new law alone has juridical force. It is difficult to fathom how the legislator will allow two parallel laws to govern the same subjects.[18] In a case on precedence the "Animadversiones" of the Sacred Congregation of the Council reveal the following pertinent statement: *"leges de praecedentia in Codice contentae sunt et apparent ex illis legibus quae 'totam de integro ordinant legis prioris materiam'* (*Canon* 22) *et ideo ad normam, Canon* 6, 1 *quaslibet leges sive particulares sive contrarias omnino abrogant."*[19] Laws wholly rearranged by the Code are classified with enactments of Canon 6, n. 1. The *"Animadversiones"* seem to place particular legislation with laws wholly recast by the Code and, therefore, according to the norms of Canon 6, n. 1, such particular laws are abrogated. The penalties of Baltimore considered above seem to be of this class; for, Canon 2319 has rearranged the legislation on penalties for attempted marriages.

The penalties in the *"Vacante Sede Apostolica"*[20] are still enforceable. This Constitution of Pius X is special legislation. All special legislation is inviolate according to the prescriptions of Canon 6, n. 5.

In the liturgical books there were some penalties annexed to specific laws. Are such abrogated by Canon 6, n. 5? In the revised edition of the *"Rituale Romanum"* the changes are made conformable to the Code. In the previous liturgical law doctors incurred a penalty who

---

16 Leech, loc. cit.

17 "Lex posterior, a competenti auctoritate lata, obrogat prori, si id expresse edicat, aut sit illi directe contraria, aut totam de integro ordinet legis prioris materiam; sed firmo praescripto can. 6, n. 1, lex generalis nullatenus derogat locorum specialium et personarum singularium statutis, nisi aliud in ipsa expresse caveatur." Canon 22.

18 Vermeersch-Creusen, op. cit., Vol. I, p. 46 Periodica, Vol. IX, 3.

19 A. A. S., Vol. XI (1919), p. 352.

20 *Codex Iuris Canonici*, Appendix, Document 1.

neglected to call a priest after three visits to the sick.[21] Another penalty was inflicted on those who did not confess and receive communion once a year. The penalty read thus "*vivus arceatur ab ecclesia, et moriens christiana careat sepultura.*"[22] The new "*Rituale Romanum*" is silent on both penalties.[23] It cannot be argued "*a posteriori*" that these, therefore, were abrogated before the revision of the Ritual. In all probability these were abolished before the new version of the Ritual appeared. Canon 2 segregates liturgical laws from the other discipline. No corrections in the rites and ceremonies of the church must be made unless the Code expressly states it. The liturgical books are sources immune from the principles of abrogation. The legislator mentions specifically that rites and ceremonies which must be observed in the celebration of the mass and in the administration of the sacraments and sacramentals are contained in the liturgical books. Such laws retain their force unless they are expressly corrected in the Code. Are the penalties attached to liturgical legislation abrogated by Canon 6, n. 5? It seems they follow the general prescriptions of Canon 6. The legislator intended to abrogate all general penal legislation. No special stipulation was made for penalties contained in the approved liturgical works. It may be legitimately inferred that liturgical prescriptions are alone secured from the determinants of Canon 2.

Definitions abound in the fifth book of the Code. This is a desirable element in any codification. Disputed points have been definitely settled by some of these definitions. Penalty today is defined: **"Poena ecclesiastica est privatio alicuius boni ad delinquentis correctionem et delicti punitionem a legitima auctoritate inflicta."** [24] In the history of Canon Law penalties were inflicted by law to make reparation for the injury. This was commonly called vindication or compensation for the crime. In the

21 *Rituale Romanum*, cap. V, tit. 4, n. 8.
22 *Rituale Romanum*, cap. IV, tit. 3, n. 1.
23 *Rituale Romanum* (the same chapters).
24 Canon 2199.

earlier history such exactions of justice existed only among private individuals. Later authority intervened to determine and moderate compensation. There was a compensation for homicide. In default of money the offender was forced to substitute animals. This objective element in addition to the subjective now constitutes the two elements necessary for inflicting a penalty; namely, the "*dolus*" and the "*damnum.*" The Romans were wont to call "*damnum*" an "*iniuria,*" i. e., "*factum contra ius.*"[25] The "*damnum*" in a crime is the detriment and perturbation caused in the social order. Not all the actions which are morally evil, nor all those which perturb society are punished, but only those which the legislator regards as dangerous to the public order. The subjective element is imputability. This ever connotes the necessity of an intelligent and free agent. Juridical imputability presupposes the moral. This is called "*dolus.*" It may be defined as "*deliberata voluntas violandi legem.*" The penalty considered is not the conventional, nor the legal, but the juridical penalty. The conventional is employed when for example they do not fulfil the obligations of a contract. The penalty imposed then is monetary. The legal obtains when authority intervenes in the same case. Juridical is the deprivation of some good be it spiritual, material or social.

The material or temporal penalty is seldom used today. In the Middle Ages bodily punishment, imprisonment, exile, confiscation of property were inflicted,[26] these, however, have long been abrogated by custom.[27] A quasi-imprisonment for unruly clerics still exists. It is a mitigation of former incarcerations. The monastery is the prison whither clerics are sent to do penance. Canon 2298, n. 8 is a restatement of the old law: "**Poenae vindicativae quae clericis tantum applicantur sunt . . . 8. Praescriptio commorandi in certo loco vel territorio.**"

25 Chelodi, *Ius Poenale*, p. 12.

26 Eichman, op. cit., p. 53; Chelodi, op. cit., p. 59.

27 Eichman, loc. cit.

The levying of fines is also expressed in the Code.[28]

The spiritual penalty is the most common. The Church as a spiritual society may withdraw or suspend access to its treasures for the betterment of the delinquent. The Church may refuse the right to christian burial, the reception of the sacraments, participation in the services. She may prohibit the right to vote in ecclesiastical elections and share in the right of benefice and office. Under given conditions these penalties are inflicted by ecclesiastical power.

Penalties are further divided into medicinal and vindictive. The medicinal is primarily directed to the correction of the delinquent. Censures are classified as medicinal penalties. Excommunication, interdict, and suspension are censures. Excommunication affects only physical persons, whilst suspension and interdict may also penalize moral persons. Excommunication and interdict also involved laics. Suspension is a clerical penalty. Interdict also is inflicted on a place. Excommunication is always a censure. Suspension and interdict may be censures or vindictive penalties. In doubt it is always presumed that the censure abides.[29] When contumacy is removed absolution of the censure may ensue. Vindictive penalties are primarily directed to the expiation of the crime. The remission of this class does not depend on the removal of contumacy,[30] but rather on the will of the superior.

The principal ways of inflicting penalties are *"latae sententiae"* and *"ferendae sententiae."* The *"poenae latae sententiae"* are incurred *"ipso facto"* when the criminal act is posited. The offender as it were pronounces judgment on himself as soon as the crime is committed. The *"poenae ferendae sententiae"* must be imposed by the judge or a competent superior.[31] Censures

---

28 Canon 2291. "Poenae vindicativae quae omnes fideles pro delictorum gravitate afficere possunt, in Ecclesia praesertim sunt: . . . . . 12. Mulcta pecuniaria."

29 Canon 2255.

30 Canon 2286.

31 Canon 2217, n. 1, § 2.

and vindictive penalties may be "*latae sententiae*" or "*ferendae sententiae.*" In civil laws "*ferendae sententiae*" alone exist. The judge is necessary for imposing the latter, whilst the legislator is indispensable for the former. In ecclesiastical law one and the same person may enact and apply the penalties. Penalties are always considered "*ferendae sententiae*" unless it is expressly stated that they are contracted "*latae sententiae*" or "*ipso facto,*" or "*ipso iure.*" Other kindred expressions may be used by the legislator with the same connotation.[32]

All these penalties of the old law are abrogated when they are not explicitly mentioned in the Code. It does not imply that the competent superiors could not annex new penal legislation. Nor does it confine the application of the penalties to those specified in the Code. Wherever the Canons do not propose the penalties "*taxative*" the Ordinary may inflict others. In the common vindictive penalties there is not a complete enumeration,[33] nor in the penitential precepts.[34] The Ordinary, however, must use the Canons involved as the basis of his action. When the word "*praesertim*" is employed in an enumeration may one conclude that some penal legislation is implicitly contained in the Code? The legislator points out the principal penalties. The Ordinary may, therefore, add others which are not mentioned in the Canon. When the legislator states that these are the chief punishments there certainly are others of less importance. This is contrary to the statements of some jurists.[35] Silence of the Code, they aver, is an argument for the abrogation of a penalty. Ablation of the law is favored even if a penalty seems to be implicitly

---

32 Canon 2217, § 2.

33 Canon 2291.

34 Canon 2313, § 1, "*Pracipuae poenitentiae sunt praecepta.*" The principal penitential precepts are: Note the difference in Canon 2306, "*Remedia poenalia sunt.*"

35 Cicognagni, Vol. II, p. 44; Perathomer, *Das Kirchliche Gesetzbuch,* p. 34; Toso, op. cit., p. 70.

contained in the Code. Therefore, penalties not explicitly nor implicitly contained in the Code are abrogated.

An instance of a penal law not explicitly nor implicitly contained in the Code is found in the *"Orientalium dignitas"*:

> "Missionarius quilibet latinus, e clero saeculari vel regulari, qui orientalem quempiam ad latinum ritum consilio auxiliove inducat, praeter suspensionem a divinis quam ipso facto incurret, ceterasque poenas per eamdem Constitutionem Demandatam inflictas, officio suo privetur et excludatur. Quae praescriptio ut certa et firma consistat, exemplar eius patere vulgatum apud Latinorum ecclesias iubemus."[36]

This penalty has been abolished by the legislator of the Code. There is no explicit nor implicit mention of it in the new law.

Penal laws found in the sources of the old law are all abolished. Those laws which are implicitly or explicitly embodied in the new legislation are not relegated to the history of Canon Law, but are retained as interpretative norms. Few penal laws have been integrally transmitted into the Code. Some are entirely new. Most of the preceding legislation on penalties has been formulated anew.[37] If Canons of the fifth book are entirely or partially constructed from the previous legislation, the antecedent enactment may be used as a norm of interpretation. In this regard the general prescriptions of Canon 6, n. 2, 3, 4, are applicable. The punishment meted out in Canon 2351 is taken from the *"Apostolicae Sedis."* An interpretation of the old law on duelling is serviceable today:

> *"Ex iure pro duello habetur et duelli poenis subiicitur, pugna illa in qua tantum sit periculum vulneris, quaeque initur cum pacto de dirimendo certamine, cum primum alteruter vulneratus fuerit seu sanguinem fuderit."*[38]

The Canonist must be ever mindful of the interpretative principles in the Code. The penal legislation in many

36 *Fontes Juris Canonici*, Vol. III, p. 456.
37 Eichman, op. cit., p. 23.
38 A. S. S., Vol. XXIII, p. 234.

instances is an exception to the general norms. The jurist, therefore, should align the interpretations of the old law wherever they are relevant and at the same time keep in mind the interpretative principles on the penal law of the Code.

Article II—Omission of Other Disciplinary Laws.

"Si qua ex ceteris disciplinaribus legibus, quae usque ad huc viguerunt, nec explicite nec implicite in Codice contineatur, ea vim omnem amisisse dicenda est, nisi in probatis liturgicis libris reperiatur, aut lex sit iuris divini sive positivi, sive naturalis." Canon 6, n. 6.

The old disciplinary enactments which are opposed to the Code, penal laws which have been omitted, and other disciplinary laws which are not explicitly nor implicitly embedded in the Code are abrogated. Exception is made for ordinances which are reserved, these remain intact. This number concludes the wholesale abrogations of the new legislation. What a contrast to the limited ablations in the past! The sweeping abrogations are of inexpressible aid to the canonist. No longer is there the appeal to an obsolete and useless law possible. This characteristic has also made the Code a monumental work.

That Canon 6 is a logical and comprehensive treatise of the relation of laws is irrefutable. Canon 6, n. 1 states the relation of laws which have the same matter but differ in form. Wherever the old legislation is substantially converted into the Canons the legislator treats of the identity of matter and form.[39] Omission of the law reveals not identity but disparity of matter and form. Laws which are not explicitly nor implicitly in the Code belong to this classification. Laws identical in matter and form, according to the other prescription of Canon 6, cannot be omitted. Diversity of form and identity of matter are the essence of opposition. Therefore, disparity is the keynote of omission.

---

39 Canon 6, n. 2.

The clause "*si qua ex ceteris legibus disciplinaribus*" deals with the remaining laws. According to Blat[40] it excludes penal laws and the enactments which are in doubtful accord with the old law. Toso[41] favors the exclusion of the penal alone. The wording of the clause is somewhat abstruse. If it refers to the various types of disciplinary laws then erstwhile laws which are not penal are here considered. If it pertains to the relation of matter in two laws, then it involves laws that are not contradictory, and enactments not integrally nor partially retained. Practically the question means nothing. Whatever the remaining laws may be, they are abrogated.

Laws which are omitted in the Code are abrogated. Maroto calls this a tacit abrogation. The legislator intended to make an integral rearrangement of Canon Law; if he neglected to do this with some law it is tacitly abrogated.[42] The entire statement of Maroto is unmindful of the primary purpose of codification. To discard the useless and obsolete was the primary intention of the legislator. This Canon was formulated with that in view and not to assuage the neglect of the legislator. Such laws are not tacitly abrogated. It is difficult to fathom a tacit abrogation. To have abrogation at any time certain principles governing it must be established by the legislator. The application of these expressed principles cannot be called tacit abrogation.

Of a certainty number 6 refers only to universal laws. The legislator in Canon 6, n. 1 makes specific prescriptions for particular legislation, whereas in number 6 they are omitted. Had the legislator intended to include particular laws he would have inserted a clause similar to the one found in Canon 6, n. 1. Canon 22 may be adduced in support of this statement: " . . . **sed firmo praescripto Can. 6, n. 1, lex generalis nullatenus derogat**

40 Blat, op. cit., p. 69.

41 Toso, op. cit., Vol. I, p. 20.

42 Maroto, op. cit., p. 158.

locorum specialium et personarum singularium statutis, nisi aliud in ipsa expresse caveatur." Wherever there is opposition of laws the particular is repealed unless, as provided in Canon 6, n. 1, mention is made to the contrary. The general does not derogate the particular unless it is expressly stated. This provision had been accepted by Boniface VIII.[43] Canon 6, n. 6 specifies nothing for particular legislation. The mind of the legislator evidently restricts number 6 to the general legislation.

How can former enactments be embodied in the Canons? Some antecedent laws are transferred verbatim into the Code. Canon 866, § 1: **Omnibus fidelibus cuiusvis ritus datur facultas, ut, pietatis causa, sacramentum Eucharisticum quolibet ritu confectum suscipiant,**" is a restatement of the Apostolic Constitution "*Tradita ab antiquis.*"[44] Legislation may be converted into Canons not in the identical but in equivalent terms. Most of the previous enactments are thus contained in the Canons. Thus Canon 2149, § 2 recasts with the same connotation a prescription of the Decree "*Maxima Cura.*"[45] Some Apostolic Constitutions are not transcribed into Canons. The substance of such legislation, however, is found in the constitution. These are equivalent to laws transcribed into the Code. Usually such legislation reads "*Ad normam constitutionum Apostolicarum.*"[46] These three classes actually exist in the Code. Such laws are explicitly contained in the new legislation.[47] What laws are implicitly embodied therein? Some Canons have prescriptions which are evidently incomplete. An instance is alleged in Canon 99:

"In Ecclesia, praeter personas physicas, sunt etiam personae morales, publica auctoritate constitutae, quae distinguuntur in personas morales collegiales et non collegiales, ut ecclesiae, Seminaria, beneficia, etc."

---

43 C. 1, de Constitutionibus, 1. 2. in VI°.
44 A. A. S., IV (1912), 616, § 3.
45 A. A. S., II (1910), 636.
46 Canon 904.
47 Vermeersch-Creusen, op. cit., p. 45.

The "*etc.*" makes allowance for other examples not mentioned in the Canon. Again prescriptions abound which are not codified "*taxative.*" Such are introduced with the word "*praesertim*:" "*Hae causae sunt praesertim,*"[48] "*poenae vindicativae quae omnes fideles pro delictorum gravitate afficere possunt, in Ecclesia praesertim sunt,*"[49] "*praecipuae poenitentiae sunt praecepta.*"[50] The most suitable definition of laws implicitly contained in the Code is given by Noval:[51] "*quae ex eo* (*Codice*) *deducuntur directe quia in lege ibidem expressa includuntur, tanquam conclusio in principio, vel species in genere, vel pars in toto, vel id quod minus in eo quod maius est.*" The types mentioned above are readily denominated by the definition. These then are implicitly contained in the Code.

Laws which are not explicitly nor implicitly contained in the Code are abrogated. The legislator, therefore, relegates them to the history of Canon Law. As ordinary interpretative sources such enactments are never used. In very rare cases will the legislator tolerate recourse to these discarded laws. Whenever there is a gap in the legislation be it general or particular, the canonist may appeal to laws enacted in similar circumstances. In such a case the old law may serve as a norm for supplying the deficient legislation.[52] With this one exception the legislator passes a final sentence on antecedent laws which have been abrogated.

A very pertinent example for the abrogation of an enactment which is not explicitly nor implicitly embodied in the Code is found in a "*Decretum*" of the Sacred Congregation of the Religious.[53] The Decree attaches

---

48 Canon 2147, § 2.

49 Canon 2291.

50 Canon 2313, § 1.

51 Noval, op. cit., p. 47.

52 Canon 20: Si certa de re desit expressum praescriptum legis sive generalis sive particularis, norma sumenda est, nisi agatur de poenis applicandis, a legibus latis in similibus; a generalibus iuris principiis cum aequitate canonica servatis; a stylo et praxi Curiae Romanae; a communi constantique sententia doctorum."

53 A. A. S., Vol. I (1908), p. 523.

special clauses to the indult of Secularization. The first four prescriptions of the "*Decretum*" are undoubtedly restated in Canon 642. The fifth prohibition is not explicitly nor implicitly converted into canons. It prohibits the "*saecularizatus*" from establishing an habitual domicile in places where formerly he resided as a religious. This portion of the Decree according to Canon 6, n. 6 is abrogated.

This is the general tenor of the Canon. Some apparent laws not inserted in the Code had caused not a little confusion in the canonical science. There was no mention of these enactments in the Code and still there was doubt of their abrogation. The Constitution "*Pascendi Dominici gregis*" and the *Motu-proprio* "*Sacrorum Antistitum*" were not mentioned in the Code. Were they abrogated? The Congregation of the Holy Office, shortly after the promulgation of the Code, issued a "*Decretum*" in which the matter was definitely settled:

> "*An praescriptiones ad duo supra memorata capita spectantes, post dictum diem festum Pentecostes, in vigore manere pergant an non?*" The question was answered: "*Praescriptiones praedictas, ob serpentes in praesenti modernisticos errores la tas, natura quidem sua, temporarias esse ac transitorias, ideoque in Codicem Juris Canonici referri non potuisse; aliunde tamen, cum virus Modernismi diffundi minime cessaverit, eas in pleno suo robore manere debere usquedum hac super re Apostolica Sedes aliter statuerit.*"[54]

These prescriptions remain intact because they are still a necessity for suppressing the virus of modernism. They are not inserted into the Code; for the new law does not consist of temporary and transitory but perpetual and permanent prescriptions.

The Decree "*Inter Reliquas*" also caused some doubt. It establishes prescriptions for religious obligated to military service. The Decree was not mentioned in the

---

[54] A. A. S., Vol. X (1918), p. 136.

Code. Was it therefore abrogated according to the Canon 6, n. 6? To which the Congregation of the Religious answered:

> "*Haec autem S. Congregatio, attenta negotii gra vitate, animadvertendum censet in Codice Juris Canonici nullam haberi potuisse rationem praefati Decreti 'Inter Reliquas,' nec ejusdem praescripta Canonibus inserta fuisse, cum idem Decretum, natura sua, ad circumstantias temporum et locorum habeat relationem, nec generalis legis ecclesiasticae rationem inducere possit.*"[55]

Former laws suited to particular circumstances and places have not the nature of general law. Therefore they are not within the scope of Canon 6, n. 6.

A dispute raged in certain circles regarding the Decree "*Spirituali Consolationi.*" The Congregation of Religious promulgated the Decree September 10, 1912. It was an extension of a privilege granted by Pius V to women of the Order of St. Dominic. Novices could thereby make profession before the termination of their novitiate. The "*Spirituali Consolationi*" extended this to all orders and congregations or religious societies. Kinane [56] classified this privilege with permissive laws. And thence concluded that Canon 6, n. 6 makes no exception for this class of legislation. It is therefore abrogated. Does this privilege by extension become a general law? The nature of the privilege was not changed by the "*Spirituali Consolationi.*" [57] It is a "*simplex extensio ad plures.*" [58] The Decree explicitly states "*pro animarum bono hoc privilegium extendere.*" [59] It is therefore a true privilege. Canon 4 and not Canon 6, n. 6 provides for this legislation.

Canonists of Germany had an extended controversy on the prohibition of wearing a beard. It was surmised that

---

55 A. A. S., Vol. XI (1919), p. 321, seq.

56 *Irish Ecclesiastical Record*, 1923, p. 413.

57 Roelker, *Principles of Privilege according to the Code of Canon Law*, p. 102.

58 Goynneche, *Commentarium Pro Religiosis*, 1923, p. 260, seq.

59 A. A. S., Vol. IV (1912), p. 589, seq.

the Ordinary could not enforce such a prohibition because it was not explicitly nor implicitly contained in the Code. The Congregation of the Council[60] gives a lengthy account of the nature of this prohibition. Summarily it deprives the prohibition of any semblance of general legislation. Canon 6, n. 6 cannot therefore be adduced in the argument. Furthermore it chides some canonists who place customs in Canon 6, n. 6. Canons 5 and 30 treat customs distinct from other general principles.

These pronouncements of the Congregations cited above caution the canonist in applying the prescriptions of Canon 6, n. 6. Temporary and transitory prescriptions, laws for determined circumstances and places, extension of privileges may have the semblance of general law. The utmost care must be used in gauging their juridical worth. Customs may at times give the appearance of written law. In all these enactments the jurist must be certain before an attempt is made to apply Canon 6, n. 6.

Article III—Liturgical Laws.

Omission, the determinant of abrogation, is not exhaustive in its extension. The legislator has made some notable exceptions to the general rule of the canon. Liturgical laws are immune from the principles of abrogation. Such laws ordinarily are not contained in the Code. Their sources are the approved liturgical books. Legislation on the ceremonies of the mass, the administration of the Sacraments and Sacramentals is not abrogated even if not explicitly nor implicitly contained in the Code. They retain their juridical force as long as they are embodied in the approved books. The penal laws related in these books are alone abolished as seen in the foregoing chapter.

---

60 A. A. S., Vol. XII (1920), p. 44, seq.

What are the approved liturgical books? The Sacred Congregation of Rites gives answer:

"Inter Libros Sacram spectantes Liturgiam, ad effectum praesentis Decreti, sequentes praecipue adnumerandi sunt:

a) Breviarium Romanum
b) Missale Romanum
c) Rituale Romanum
d) Pontificale Romanum

} eorumque excerpta

e) Martyrologium Romanum
f) Caeremoniale Episcoporum
g) Propria tum Officiorum, tum Missarum alicuius Diocesis, Ordinis, seu Congregationis Religiosae.
h) Memoriale Rituum Benedicti Papae XIII pro minoribus Ecclesiis.
i) Instructio Clementina pro expositione Sanctissimi Sacramenti.
j) Collectio Decretorum Sacrae Rituum Congregationis"[61]

Article IV—Natural Law.

Canon 6 is indeed comprehensive in its prescriptions. All possible classes of laws enforced in the old legislation are duly considered. Divine laws, be they positive or natural, are ultimately arrayed in this Canon. Such laws ever remain unchanged. Canon 6, n. 6 therefore, merely restates an unassailable principle of immemorable standing.

Law is commonly divided into four kinds: the eternal, the natural, the divine positive, and the human. The eternal is the law of God directing the universe to its end, which is God himself.[62] The eternal is prior to all legislation. Like the natural law its nature is a directing principle; for, it directs things to their end. As existing in God the supreme law is eternal; as it is in the subjects ruled it is known as the natural law. In essence the eternal is prior to the natural. The natural however, is first in the order of our knowledge. From the existence of

---

61 A. A. S., Vol. III (1911), p. 243.

62 Cronin, *The Science of Ethics,* Vol. 1, p. 604; Cavagnis, *Institutiones Iuris Publici Ecclesiastici,* Vol. I, p. 4.

the universe one may argue to the existence of the eternal law.[63]

The natural law is defined as the rational creature's participation in the eternal law.[64] It is a universal norm of action. All people of the earth have natural appetites which are governed by some precepts. The will has good for its object, wherefore the precept "good is to be done." This, as the habit of first principles, is inherent in all men. The natural law is also invariable in its first fundamental principles. Never can there be an abrogation of this law. What is of necessity today in the natural law cannot cease to be necessary. The primary principles never change, they are immutable.[65] Reason dictates that God cannot simultaneously will two contradictory propositions. The eternal law is unchangeable. The natural law is creature's participation in that law. Since the eternal is immutable so is its complement, the natural law. Deductions from these primary principles are called secondary precepts of the natural law. The latter have suffered some change, but the law always remained unmolested. The obligation of the law ceased but the matter remained. The Church therefore cannot change the natural law as stated in Canon 6, n. 6. She is empowered as a perfect society to declare and interpret its precepts. In a very extended sense she can dispense from those precepts whose particular obligations depend on the human will as vows and oaths.[66] In no way is she commissioned to abrogate the principles of the natural law.

Article V—The Divine Positive Laws.

The Divine Positive Law is a group of ordinances enacted by God and made known to man through revelation.[67] The Mosaic legislation was substantially abrogated. Its substitute, the evangelical law, may be divided

63 Cronin, op. cit., p. 607.
64 St. Thomas, *Summa Theologica* Prima Secundae, Questio XCIV, art. V.
65 Devoti, *Institutionum Canonicorum*, tom. I, p. 26.
66 Noldin, Vol. I, p. 139.
67 *Catholic Encyclopedia*, Vol. IX, p. 70.

into dogmatic laws or dogmas and disciplinary precepts or laws. Christ revealed many new dogmas "in the fulness of time." These constituted in part the deposit of faith. Not a few of these dogmas were defined by the Church in the course of time. The disciplinary precepts, as of old, may be divided into the moral, the ceremonial, and the judicial. The moral are those precepts of the natural law which were confirmed by Christ, as unity and indissolubility of marriage.[68] Christ introduced some moral precepts entirely new, as the administration and the reception of the sacraments.[69] The Ceremonial precepts treat of the substantial elements of the Mass and the Sacraments. Lastly, the judicial define the essential constitution of the Church and the fundamental principles of ecclesiastical rule.[70]

The divine law of its very nature is indispensable and perpetual. The legislative power was granted to the Church for the edification and not destruction[71] of the positive divine law. Its function is the determination, the protection, and observation of the divine law. An attempt to abrogate the divine law would defeat the very purpose of the legislative power. Canon 6, n. 6 restates a fundamental principle that the divine positive and natural law are immune from the determinants of abrogation.

---

68 Leitner, *Handbuch des Katholischen Kirchenrechts*, Vol. I, p. 8; Maroto, op. cit., p. 23.

69 Maroto, op. cit., p. 23.

70 Maroto, op. cit., p. 23, seq.

71 Wernz, op. cit., Vol. II, p. 167; Aichner, *Compendium Juris Ecclesiastici*, p. 103.

CHAPTER VII

THE OLD LAW AS INTERPRETER OF CANONS.

Article I. In Substantial Concordance of Laws.

"Canones qui ius vetus ex integro referunt, ex veteris iuris auctoritate, atque ideo ex receptis apud probatos auctores interpretationibus sunt aestimandi." Canon 6, § 2.

The determinants of abrogation thrust not a little erstwhile legislation into the history of Canon Law. Some of these effete enactments, however, may become serviceable wherever the present law is deficient.[1] On the other hand much of the former discipline has been retained. Very few canons are destitute of some former prescription. These old laws have juridical force only inasmuch as they are embodied in the Canons. They are the interpretative norms of the new law whenever the new and the old coincide. To establish these norms and ascertain their value is the purpose of this chapter.

"Ius vetus" Blat avers is custom and especially written law.[2] The legislator segregated customs from the written law in no uncertain terms.[3] *"Ius vetus"* refers to the laws effective at the promulgation of the Code. These are usually cited in the footnotes of each Canon. The notation of the sources, however, is not authentic. Consequently other sources may be used by the canonist provided they have survived the principles of abrogation and produce relevant matter. Thanks to the eminent canonist Gasparri not a little chaotic interpretation has been averted through the alignment of the sources under each Canon.

1 Canon 20.
2 Blat., op. cit., p. 68.
3 Canon 5.

There are Canons which reproduce the old law in its entirety. This may happen in several ways as stated above. Canons may restate the old law verbatim Canon 866, § 1, recasts word for word the third paragraph of "*Tradita ab antiquis.*"[4] Again, Canons may mention the substance of the subject-matter and immediately add the clause "ad normam Constitutionis." Canons 904 and 884 give nothing but a reference to the Constitution of Benedict XIV "*Sacramentum Poenitentiae.*"[5] They merely refer to the integral legislation on solicitation and absolution of accomplices. A third-class expresses the anterior enactment in different terminology. This is the most common form of integral conversion of the old law. The codifiers had for their objective a succinct and pithy systematization of the law. It was necessary, therefore, to cast aside the narrative and also the dilated dispositive part of the former discipline. Such reconstruction necessitated a change in the terminology. An example of this class may be adduced from Canon 2149 § 2. It has the same connotation as a prescription of the "*Maxima Cura.*"[6]

The old legislation of itself has no juridical value today. As a subsidiary source of the new law it may be used as an interpreter. Even in this capacity it is destitute of legal value unless the Code has embodied it in Canons.[7] When the legislator speaks of the "*auctoritas*" in antecedent legislation he refers to its evaluation and intrinsic worth. It is the sum and substance which the mind of the legislator reveals. The juridical terminology, the object, the adjuncts, and the context of the law all manifest the mind of the legislator.[8] In addition to these requisites the word "*auctoritas*" includes the interpretations of the old legislation, for this is another form of disclosing the legislator's mind.

---

4 A. A. S., Vol. IV (1912), p. 616, § III.
5 *Codex Juris Canonici*, Appendix. Documentum V.
6 A. A. S., Vol. II (1910), p. 581.
7 Perathoner, op. cit., p. 35.
8 Cocchi, op. cit., p. 111.

Interpretation is defined as a declaration or explanation of the genuine sense of the law.[9] Its object is to seek out and determine the exact meaning of the enactment. Of old the jurists distinguished between a mere declaration and the interpretation of the law.[10] The declaration today is called comprehensive interpretation. Its scope is not to change the law but determines the sense of the law comprehended therein from the beginning. Therefore, it adds or subtracts nothing from the original meaning. The comprehensive interpretation is also called the literal in contradistinction to the suppletive.[11] The former adds nothing anew but explains more and more the significance attached to the words. The suppletive interpretation supplies what was defective in the law. It makes additions not only to the letter of the law but also extends its scope to other circumstances. The suppletive is divided into the extensive and the restrictive. The former declares that some case is contained in the law although it is not included in its wording. Not only is it a departure from the actual meaning of the enactment but it also implies a change in the legislative mind.[12] The word *posterity* would be an extensive interpretation of *children.*[13] A restrictive interpretation declares that a case is not comprehensive though the general tenor of the law would include it. The word *children* would be a restrictive or coarctative interpretation of posterity.

The authentic interpreter in ecclesiastical legislation is the supreme legislator, the Sovereign Pontiff. The Roman Congregations have been deputed by the Pope to interpret laws. Their declarations and resolutions are authentic. A declaration or comprehensive interpretation has the force of law, and is retroactive. This is restated in the Canon 17, § 2 of the new Code: ". . . **et si verba legis in se certa declaret tantum, promulgatione non eget et valet retrorsum.**" The Congregations had

---

9 Cicognani, op. cit., p. 116.
10 Wernz, op. cit., p. 149.
11 Icard, op. cit., p. 58, seq.
12 Roelker, op. cit., p. 70.
13 Haring, *Grundzüge des Katholischen Kirchenrechtes,* Teil 1, p. 35.

this power long before the promulgation of the Code. The Sacred Congregation of the Council was proclaimed the official interpreter of the Council of Trent in disciplinary matters. What was necessary that its interpretations be declared authentic? The customary seal, with the signature of the Cardinal prefect and the Secretary of the Congregation was sufficient. The value of decrees and responses emanating from the Sacred Congregation of Rites was expressed in the following response:

> "S. R. C. 23 Maii 1846—*An decreta a Sacra Rituum Congregatione emanata, et responsiones quaecumque ab ipsa propositis dubiis scripto formiter editae, eamdem habeant auctoritatem ac si immediate ab ipso Summo Pontifice promanarent, quamvis nulla facta fuerit de iisdem relatio Sanctitati Suae.*
>
> *R. Sacra Rituum Congregatio, ad Vaticanum subsignata die coadunata in ordinario Coetu, audito a subscripto Secretario fideli relatione, expositisque rationum momentis, et diligenter consideratis, rescribendum censuit: 'Affirmative.' Atque ita rescripsit.*" [14]

The Sacred Congregation for the Propagation of the Faith gave a similar response:

> "S. C. de Propag. Fide 30 Julii 1652 (Congr. Gen. coram SSmo.) *Referente Emo. D Card Cesio litteras Fr. Antonii a S. Maria Ord. strictioris observ. S. Francisci, et Praefecti Missionis Sinarum Ordinis eiusdem scribentis ab insulis Philippinis esse ibi aliquos religiosos qui parvipendentes decreta S. Congregationis de Prop. Fide cum maximo animarum praeiudicio, spargunt per illas partes resolutiones et decreta praefatae S. Congregationis facere tantum opinionem probabilem, uti puram et simplicem Cardinalium declarationem unde posse etiam contrarium, defendi, SSmus. D. N. (Innocentius X) confirmavit decretum S. M. Urbani VIII, videlicet quod decreta S. Congregationis Generalis de Prop. Fide quotiescumque sint a Praefecto eiusdem firmata, a Secretario subscripta, et sigillo munita, vim et valorem habeant Constitutionis Apostolicae, ac ab omnibus et singulis inviolabiliter serventur.*" [15]

---

[14] *Collectanea*, n. 1006.
[15] *Collectanea*, n. 119.

Capello[16] rightly concludes that this Congregation as the rest is a veritable organ of the Pontiff and, therefore, its responses must be accepted as if given by the Pontiff. In the declarations, responses and resolutions of these Congregations the authenticity cannot be challenged. The respective Congregations must ever remain within their jurisdiction.

How can a declaration or comprehensive interpretation be distinguished from the extensive and restrictive? It seems that the individual canonist can gauge the quality of interpretation from the sense of the response. The Sacred Congregation of the Council uses the phrase "*facto verbo cum SSmo*" and kindred clauses. This expresses a change or an extension of the law.[17] The same may be said of the responses of other congregations. The comprehensive then will have no clause appended. This seems conclusive from the spirit of the legislation. The declaration is not in need of promulgation. The others must be promulgated and, therefore, the approbation of the pontiff is attached. Canon 17 restates the same thought.

Besides the authentic there is also the doctrinal, the usual and the judicial interpretation. The judicial is restricted to the cases over which the judge has jurisdiction. The usual interpretation is that which has been introduced by custom. The doctrinal according to Canon 6, n. 2 exacts specific consideration. The doctrinal interpretation is made by men who are eminent jurists. Ordinarily every private individual may interpret laws according to the rules of jurisprudence, unless a special prohibition has been made. All forms of interpretation on the decrees of the Council of Trent were prohibited by Pius IV.[18] The Code in Canon 6, n. 2 bids us have recourse to the doctrine of the approved authors. The authentic, however, always remains the guide for the doctrinal.

---

16 Capello, *De Curia Romana,* Vol. I, p. 241.
17 Wernz, op. cit., p. 173 (footnotes).
18 Schmalzgrueber, op. cit., p. 215.

Of old there existed declarations and interpretations of the law. These were glosses usually explaining the words or the text. A methodical system was developed in the early days of jurisprudence. The school of Law at Bologna records a prospering school of interpretation.[19] When the "*Decretum Gratiani*" was published the jurists turned their efforts to canonical legislation. The interpreter of the Roman Law was called "*legista*" whilst in Canon Law he was called "*decretista*" or "*decretalista.*"[20] In the classical epoch of Canon Law the doctors came into prominence. This period is commonly dated from the 16th Century to the 18th inclusive. There were then many eminent doctors of the law. These institututed what is termed the "*schola textus*" which later developed into the "*institutiones.*" In our time another school has been added "*schola iuris publici ecclesiastici.*"[21]

Who are the approved authors in our day? Negatively they are not the authors whose works have been condemned, e. g. Van Espen. His works, "*Opcra Omnia;*" were placed on the Index November 18, 1732, by the Congregation of the Holy Office.[22] From a positive standpoint, approved jurists are principally those who have been used and quoted by the Roman Curia. True, there is not an official list of canonists. A sanction, however, is attached to the authors quoted freely by the Roman Congregations and Tribunals. The writer has drawn up a list of such jurists. The authors catalogued below have been used by the Roman Curia to interpret the old legislation which is embodied in the Code. The jurists marked with an asterisk have been used elsewhere in the dissertation. Their works are not mentioned below, for they are embodied in the general bibliography. The date and place of some few publications are omitted in

19 Haring, op. cit., p. 115.

20 Haring, loc. cit.; Maroto, op. cit., p. 103.

21 Maroto, op. cit., p. 107, seq.

22 *Index Librorum Prohibitorum Leonis XIII Cum Pontificis Auctoritate Recognitus SSMI. D. N. Pii XI*, p. 275.

the syllabus; for, these works were not available at the time. The writer has confined this survey to a period dating from 1918 to 1924 inclusive:

De Herdt, P. J.,[23] Praxis Capitularis, Lovanii, 1881.
Ceccoperius,[24] Lucubrationes canonicae.
Scaccia, R.,[25] Tractatus de Appellationibus, Coloniae, 1717.
Aichner, S.[26]
Engel, L.,[27] Collegium Universi Juris Canonici, Beneventi, 1760.
Rosset, M.,[28] Theologia Dogmatico-moralis, Camberri, 1876.
Scherer, R.,[29] Handbuch des Kirchenrecht, Lipsiae, 1898.
Ballerini-Palmieri,[30] Opus Theologicum Morale, Prati, 1889.
Fejc,[31] De Impedimentis Matrimonii.
Lotterius, M.,[32] De Beneficiariis, Patavii, 1700.
*Barbosa, A.[33]
Cosci, C.,[34] De Separatione Thori, 1773.
Pontius, B.,[35] De Sacramento Matrimonii, Bruxellis, 1627.
Lugo,[36] De Justitia et Jure.
Konings-Putzer,[37] Commentarium in Facultates Apostolicas.
*Suarez.[38]
Many, S.,[39] De Missa Romae, 1903.
Genarri, C.,[40] Consultazioni Morali, canonische e liturgische, Rome.
Pallotini, S.,[41] Collectio. omnium conclusionum et resolutionum quae in causis propositis apud S. C. Concilii Trid. interpretum Romae, 1868-1893.
Benedict XIV,[42] Consultationes Canonicae et Morales, Romae, 1884.

---

23 A. A. S., Vol. X (1918), p. 63.
24 A. A. S., Vol. X (1918), p. 37.
25 A. A. S., Vol. X (1918), p. 33.
26 A. A. S., Vol. XI (1919), p. 157.
27 A. A. S., Vol. XI (1919), p. 156.
28 A. A. S., Vol. XI (1919), p. 156.
29 A. A. S., Vol. XI (1919), p. 90.
30 A. A. S., Vol. XI (1919), p. 90.
31 A. A. S., Vol. XI (1919), p. 90.
32 A. A. S., Vol. XI (1919), p. 79.
33 A. A. S., Vol. XI (1919), p. 79.
34 A. A. S., Vol. XI (1919), p. 197.
35 A. A. S., Vol. XI (1919), p. 293.
36 A. A. S., Vol. XI (1919), p. 293.
37 A. A. S., Vol. XII (1920), p. 539.
38 A. A. S., Vol. XI (1919), p. 293.
39 A. A. S., Vol. XII (1920), p. 539.
40 A. A. S., Vol. XII (1920), p. 539.
41 A. A. S., Vol. XII (1920), p. 446.
42 A. A. S., Vol. ⅩII (1920), p. 446.

*St. Thomas.[43]
Stremler,[44] Traité des peines ecclesiastiques.
Garcia, N.,[45] De Beneficiis Ecclesiasticis, Venetiis, 1618.
Vecchiotti, J.,[46] Institutiones Canonicae, Augustae Taurinorum, 1875.
Lucidi, A.,[47] De Visitatione Sac. Liminum, Romae, 1883.
*Leurenio.[48]
Pignatelli, J.,[49] Consultationes Canonicae, Coloniae, 1700.
Salzano, T. O. P.,[50] Lezioni di Diritto Canonico.
Fagnanus, P.,[51] Commentarium in Libros Decretalium, Venitiis, 1729.
Viviani, J.,[52] Praxis Juris Patronatus, Venitiis, 1652.
Pitonius, J.,[53] Disceptationes Ecclesiasticae, Venitiis, 1733.
Sincero,[54] Conclusiones Comissionis Episcopalis.
Berardi, C.,[55] Commentarium in Jus Ecclesiasticum Universum.
DeFargua,[56] Commentarium in singulas canones de Jure Patronatu.
Sebastianelli, G.,[57] Praelectiones Juris Canonici, Romae, 1908.
Bouix, D.,[58] De Principiis Juris Canonici, Parisiis, 1882.
*Vering.[59]
*Icard.[60]
Müller, A.,[61] Lexicon des Kirchenrechts, Wurz, 1841.
Smith, W.,[62] Elements of Ecclesiastical Law, New York, 1880.
*Pirhing.[63]
*Schmalzgrueber.[64]

---

43 A. A. S., Vol. XI (1919), p. 195.
44 A. A. S., Vol. XII (1920), p. 362.
45 A. A. S., Vol. XII (1920), p. 358.
46 A. A. S., Vol. XII (1920), p. 130.
47 A. A. S., Vol. XII (1920), p. 90.
48 A. A. S., Vol. XIII (1921), p. 512.
49 A. A. S., Vol. XIII (1921), p. 394.
50 A. A. S., Vol. XIII (1921), p. 394.
51 A. A. S., Vol. XIII (1921), p. 267.
52 A. A. S., Vol. XIII (1921), p. 65.
53 A. A. S., Vol. XIII (1921), p. 65.
54 A. A. S., Vol. XIII (1921), p. 63.
55 A. A. S., Vol. XIII (1921), p. 62.
56 A. A. S., Vol. XIII (1921), p. 62.
57 A. A. S., Vol. XIII (1921), p. 49.
58 A. A. S., Vol. XIII (1921), p. 45.
59 A. A. S., Vol. XIII (1921), p. 44.
60 A. A. S., Vol. XIII (1921), p. 44.
61 A. A. S., Vol. XIII (1921), p. 44.
62 A. A. S., Vol. XIII (1921), p. 44.
63 A. A. S., Vol. XIV (1922), p. 655.
64 A. A. S., Vol. XIV (1922), p. 655.

Lega, M.,[65] Praelectiones in Textum Juris Canonici, Romae, 1905.
D'Angelis, P.,[66] Praelectiones Juris Canonici, Romae, 1877.
D'Annibale, J.,[67] Summula Theologiae Moralis, Romae, 1897.
Gasparri, P.,[68] De Matrimonio, Parisiis, 1894.
Sanchez, T.,[69] De Sancto Matrimonii Sacramento, Antverpiae 1626.
Oijetti, B.,[70] Synopsis Rerum Moralium, Romae, 1912.
Pichler, R. P.,[71] Epitome Juris Canonici, Venitiis, 1755.
Ferraris, L. O. F. M.,[72] Prompta Bibliotheca Canonica, Parisiis, 1865.
Santi, F.,[73] Praelectiones Juris Canonici, Ratisbonae, 1886.
Cencius, L.,[74] De Censibus, Lugduni, 1730.
*Wernz.[75]
*Reiffenstuel.[76]
Genicot, E.,[77] Institutiones Theologia Moralis, Bruxellis, 1922.

This list is by no means exhaustive. Other authors who have received the same sanction in the old law may be numbered amongst the approved jurists. Whenever the old legislation is converted into the canons of the Code the interpreters of the former law become very serviceable.

Why has the legislator recognized doctrinal interpretation in the Code? Very often the law is obscure and apparently ambiguous. The legislator has given no authentic interpretation to the text or the context. To reach the legislator for consultation is utterly impossible. Under such circumstances canonists have access to an interpretation other than the authentic, namely, the doctrinal.[78]

---

65 A. A. S., Vol. XIV (1922), p. 654.
66 A. A. S., Vol. XIV (1922), p. 515.
67 A. A. S., Vol. XIV (1922), p. 514.
68 A. A. S., Vol. XIV (1922), p. 514.
69 A. A. S., Vol. XIV (1922), p. 475.
70 A. A. S., Vol. XIV (1922), p. 475.
71 A. A. S., Vol. XV (1923), p. 517.
72 A. A. S., Vol. XV (1923), p. 517.
73 A. A. S., Vol. XV (1923), p. 517.
74 A. A. S., Vol. XVI (1924), p. 475.
75 A. A. S., Vol. XVI (1924), p. 478.
76 A. A. S., Vol. XVI (1924), p. 479.
77 A. A. S., Vol. XVI (1924), p. 480.
78 Schmalzgrueber, op. cit., p. 215.

Article II. Partial Concordance of Laws.

"Canones qui ex parte tantum cum veteri jure congruunt, qua congruunt, ex iure antiquo aestimandi sunt; qua discrepant, sunt ex ipsorum sententia dijudicandi." Canon 6, n. 3.

In the preface to the Code Cardinal Gasparri prepares the canonist for this prescription of Canon 6: *"Vix animadvertere attinet, canones haud semper cum suis fontibus omni ex parte in sententia congruere."* Canons abound in which the old is partially embodied whilst a new prescription substitutes that part of the old which has been derogated. It was the purpose of the legislator to rejuvenate what was useful in the old law and to discard the obsolete and the useless. *"Quia utile per inutile non debet vitiari?"* a juridical axiom,[79] is well applied here. Where such a conflict of the laws would exist the legislator has supplied rules of interpretation. This is the purpose of Canon 6, n. 3. Wherever canons agree with the old enactments, the old is the interpreter; wherever a discrepancy abides the prescription is interpreted according to the norms of the new law. The Canons which agree with the old are interpreted according to the rules determined by Canon 6, n. 2.

Discrepancy is a prerequisite for Canon 6, n. 3. It implies a state of dissimilarity or discordance with another legislation. Canon 6, n. 1, proposed principles for substantial opposition in the laws. In Canon 6, n. 2 the legislator adopted interpretative norms for substantial concordance of the two laws. Canon 6, n. 3 deals with partial agreement and partial conflict. Partial concordance of laws in the canons employs the interpretative rules of Canon 6, n. 2. Discrepancy implies two juridical elements: derogation and obrogation. The former *"ipso facto"* displaces the discordant prescription of the old law, whilst the latter is the introduction of the new law.

---

[79] Layman, *Theologia Moralis,* Lib. 1, Tract IV, cap. XXII.

This seems to militate against a quondam opinion: "*Semper lex nova, si per contrarietatem fieri possit, secundum antiquam interpretari debet, etiam verbis aliquando acceptis in sensu minus proprio.*"[80]

There are several ways of applying Canon 6, n. 3. Whenever the nature of the old enactment is kept intact but the extension of the law has been changed, Canon 6, n. 3 may be invoked. The Impediment of Disparity of Cult is basically identical with the former legislation. The extension of the impediment has changed. Formerly disparity of cult existed between the baptized Catholic or non-Catholic and a non-baptized person. Today it affects marriages between the non-baptized and a person baptized in the Catholic Church or converted thereto from heresy or schism. In this case the nature of the law is in accord with former legislation and, therefore, is interpreted in the light of the old norms. The extension, however, manifests a discrepancy. It is, therefore, interpreted according to the juridical significance of the new law.

Contrarywise Canons may contain prescriptions where the nature of the old law is entirely changed, then the extension and the accidentals must follow the nature. The accessory follows the principal in abrogation. In a substantial change of anything, the accidents vanish with the substantial form. Accidents of the new substance may be similar to those of the old substance, but their value emanates from the new and not the old, so too in law. When an enactment submits to a substantial change the accidents follow the substance. But this is not applicable *vice versa*. Accidents may change whilst the substance remains the same. This is the form of mutation found in the foregoing paragraph. Where the substance of the law is rearranged how are the accidentals or the extension to be interpreted? The rules of Canon 18 are employed which are treated at length in this chapter.

Wherever there is concordance between the old law

80 Schmalzgrueber, op. cit., p. 216.

and the canon the rules of Canon 6, n. 2 are invoked. In discrepancy, however, the new law is adjudicated in a sense proper to itself,[81] "*ex sua ipsorum sententia dijudicandi sunt.*" The word "*ipsorum*" refers to "*Canones.*" The significance of the canon is the interpretative norm.

An authentic interpretation,[82] be it "*per modum legis*" or otherwise,[83] gives the official significance of the prescription. When there is no official declaration Canon 18 and the other rules of interpretation in the Code are applicable. The writer must confine himself to the general tenor of Canon 18; for the significance of the canons extends thruout the Code.

"Leges ecclesiasticae intelligendae sunt secundum propriam verborum significationem in textu et contextu consideratam; quae si dubia et obscura manserit, ad locos parallelos, si qui sint, ad legis finem ac circumstantias et ad mentem legislatoris est recurrendum." Canon 18.

The first consideration is the study of the terminology. Words are the human means of conveying thought. The legislator manifests his mind thru words. The juridical terminology ought to have common grounds both for the subject and the legislator. If the legislator has defined something anew in the Code there can be no recourse to the traditional signification of the same word. The legislator, as an instance has defined the word "*vagus,*"[84] "*officium,*"[85] "*ordinarius*"[86] and "*poena.*"[87] In such instances the common jurisprudence cannot be employed. The usual significance of words is not the philological or the etymological meaning but it is taken from contemporary writers, juridical lexicons, and speech common

---

81 Pöschl, *Kurzgefastes Lehrbuch des Katholischen Kirchenrechtes,* p. 47.

82 The Pontifical Commission for the Interpretation of the Code is the official interpreter today. Cf. "*Cum Juris Canonici*" in the beginning of the Code.

83 Canon 17.

84 Canon 91.

85 Canon 145.

86 Canon 198.

87 Canon 2215.

at the time. DeMeester [88] offers a very appropriate example. The word *"censèmus"* today expresses a mere opinion. In the time of the Decretals it implied a precept. Whenever the legislator has not defined a word in the Code it is presumed that there is no deviation from its usual meaning.

Terminology clear from a new definition or from the accepted meaning needs no interpretation. If there is some equivocation or obscurity the significance may be gleaned from the context. The interpretation should avoid a digression from the sense of the common law. The legislator is presumed to use the customary terms until the contrary is established.[89] The definitions of the Code must not be urged against the context. The legislator seems to imply this in two passages. Canon 145 defines ecclesiastical office in a strict and in a broad sense. The strict should be émployed unless the context reveals otherwise. Again in Canon 488, § 7 the "**moniales**" are defined "**religiosae votorum solemnium aut nisi ex rei natura vel ex contextu sermonis aliud constet, religiosae quarum vota ex instituto sunt solemnia. . . .**"

If the text and the context do not warrant certitude and clarity the legislator proffers other means of attaining them, "**ad locos parallelos, si qui sint . . . recurrendum.**" The canons sometimes refer to parallel passages in the Code, viz; Canons 136 and 2379. Canons have prescriptions which are applicable to parallel passages of other canons. Canon 88 defines the word "impubes." Canon 2230 uses the same word in the sense defined in Canon 88: "Parallel texts are such as have an affinity with the subject or rather expressly related to the same."[90]

The legislator proposes another method when the above are not serviceable: "**ad finem ac circumstantias legis . . . est recurrendum.**" The end or purpose of the law is the

---

88 DeMeester, op. cit., p. 180, footnote n. 1.

89 DeMeester, op. cit., p. 180; c. 8 de verb. sign. V, 40 in VI°. *"Propterea, si prolixam epistolam meam ad interpretandum accipere te fortasse contigerit, rogo non verbum ex verbo, sed sensum ex sensu transferri: quia plerumque dum proprietas verborum attenditur, sensus veritatis amittitur."*

90 Augustine, op. cit., p. 97.

reason which motivated the legislator to enact it. It is distinct from the law. In this connection the juridical axiom "*Ubi eadem est ratio, ibi eadem debet esse juris dispositio*" may be used. The legislator may allege some reason for the existence of a law but seldom are the integral cause, the total end, and all the reasons expressed. Whatever reasons are known may be used as interpretative norms. The circumstances of a law accommodate it to persons, places and times. To illustrate this point: Were a Circular Letter sent out by the Congregation of the Council enjoining all clerics to wear the "*vestis talaris*" at all times, the clergy of the United States would not be affected; for the "*vestis talaris*" is not our street garb.

Lastly, the mind of the legislator is commonly known thru the text and context, thru the end and circumstances of the law. The legislator may disclose his mind privately, or thru individuals who collaborated in the codification, or thru those who prepared and wrote the law.[91] "If all the means so far enumerated fail in discovering the true mind of the legislator, nothing is left but to make direct inquiry by petitioning the competent authority."[92]

---

91 Vermeersch-Creusen, op. cit., p. 70.
92 Augustine, op. cit., p. 98.

CHAPTER VIII.

DOUBT OF DISCREPANCY IN LAWS.

Canon 6, n. 4:

"In dubio num aliquid canonum praescriptum cum iure discrepet, a veteri iure non est recendum."

Contrariety which is certain and substantial abrogates a prior law. Partial discrepancy which is evident derogates the antecedent enactment. Whenever contrariety or discrepancy is only apparent a reconciliation should be effected. In support of this statement Reiffenstuel[1] quotes a juridical aphorism, *"expedit concordare iura iuribus et eorum correctiones evitare."* The Code presents a more definite rule. When it is doubtful whether a prescription of a canon disagrees with the old, the latter must be upheld. In doubt the presumption is in favor of the former legislation. The presumption is merely in favor of a more seasoned rule of interpretation. It is not the rejuvenation of the old law but merely an appeal to an interpretation which is certain. If the opposite were favored much confusion would ensue as evinced in the foregoing article. When, however, the legislator prefers the old established rules, be they authentic or doctrinal, not a little trouble is avoided for the jurist.

What kind of doubt is necessary to warrant this conclusion? Negative doubt fluctuates between two opposites. It is practically destitute of a reason for affirming or denying. In practise this redounds to ignorance and therefore must be rejected. Positive doubt exists when there is a well founded reason for affirming now and again denying but the reasons more or less mutually destroy their initial force. Since the motives are nearly equal

1 Reiffenstuel, op. cit., p. 119, n. 492.

both judgments of the mind may be called opinions.[2] It is not necessary to mention this distinction to conscientious jurists; but since the law considers all mental states it is not amiss to mention this here.

Vermeersch would divide not doubt but discrepancy into positive and negative. Positive discrepancy obtains whenever a canon prescribes or prohibits something other than the old law. Negative discrepancy if a prescription or prohibition of the old law is neither explicitly nor implicitly contained in the new law.[3] The former may be contrariety or some enactment entirely new. If it is entirely new there can be no discrepancy. Negative discrepancy is defined as omission. This is provided for in Canon 6, n. 6. It seems a principle of division is violated "*Nullum membrum divisionis excedat totum divisum.*" Discrepancy implies conflict, opposition, or disagreement of the two enactments. Omission does not convey these ideas; for, it is not at variance with present legislation which is provided for in Canon 6, n. 1 and n. 3.

Wherever there is positive doubt of a discrepancy the old law is favored as the interpretative norm. The canonist therefore must follow the general rules adopted in Canon 6, n. 2.

---

2 Cicognani, op. cit., p. 43; Toso, op. cit., p. 42.
3 Vermeersch-Creusen, op. cit., p. 44.

SOURCES.

Acta Apostolicae Sedis, Romae, 1909.
Acta Apud Sanctam Sedem, Romae, 1865-1870.
Acta Sanctae Sedis, Romae, 1870-1908.
Acta et Decreta Con. Plen. Balt. 111, Baltimorae, 1886.
Codex Juris Canonici, Romae, 1918.
Collectanea S. C. de Propaganda Fide, Romae, 1907.
Corpus Juris Canonici, Lipsiae, 1922.
Corpus Juris Civilis, Berlin, 1895.
Fontes Juris Canonici, Romae, 1923-1926.
Rituale Romanum, Ratisbonae, 1895.
Rituale Romanum, Turonibus, 1925.

BIBLIOGRAPHY.

Aichner, Dr. Simon, Compendium Juris Canonici, Brixiae, 1887.

Archiv für Katholisches Kirchenrecht, Mainz, 1918.

Augustine, Charles, O. S. B., A Commentary on the New Code of Canon Law, 4 ed., St. Louis, 1921.

Barbosa, Augustinus, Tractatus Varii, Lugduni, 1660.

Bargilliat, M., Praelectiones Juris Canonici, Parisiis, 1923.

Benedict XIV (Prosper Lambertini), De Synodo Dioecesana, Romae, 1806.

Berneregqi, Dott. A., Methodi e Sistemi Delle Antiche Collezione e Del Nuovo Codice Di Diritto Canonico, Monza, 1919.

Blat, Albertus, O. P., Commentarium in Textum Juris Canonici, Romae, 1921.

Bouix, D., Tractatus de Papa, Parisiis, 1869.

Capello, Felix, M., S. J., De Matrimonio, Taurinorum Augustae, 1923.

Capello, Felix, M., S. J., De Curia Romana, Romae, 1911.

Catholic Encyclopedia, New York, 1907-1912.

Cavagnis, Felix, S., Institutiones Juris Publici Ecclesiastici, Romae, 1882.

Cerato, Prosdocimus, Censurae Vigentes, Patavii, 1921.

Chelodi, Ioannes, Jus Poenale, Tridenti, 1925.

Cicognani, Hamletus, Jus Canonicum, Romae, 1925.

Cocchi, Guidus, C. M., Commentarium in Codicem Juris Canonici, Taurinorum Augustae, 1921.

Commentarium pro Religiosis, Romae, 1923.

Cronin, Michael, The Science of Ethics, Dublin, 1909.

DeMeester, A., Compendium Juris Canonici et Juris Civilis, Brugis, 1921.

Denzinger, H., Enchiridion Symbolorum, (edit. XIII quam paravit Clemens Bannwart, S. J.), Albany, 1907.

Devoti, Joannes, Institutionum Canonicarum, Leodii, 1833.

Eichman, Edwardus, Das Strafrecht des Codex Juris Canonici, Paderborn, 1920.

Falco, Mario, Introduzione Allo Studio Del Codex Juris Canonici, Torino, 1925.

Funk, F. X., A Manual of Church History, St. Louis, Mo.

Haring, J. B., Grundzüge des Katholischen Kirchenrechts, Graz, 1924.

Hefele, Carl Josef von, Conciliengeschichte, Freiburg, 1873-1890.

Hergenroether-Kirsch, Handbuch der Allgemeinen Kirchengeschichte, Freiburg, 1911-1917.

Hermann, R. P. J., C. SS. R., Institutiones Theologiae Dogmaticae, Romae, 1914.

Hilling N. Allgemeine Normen, Mainz, 1926.

Homiletic Review, New York, 1924.

Icard, J., S. S., Praelectiones Juris Canonici, Paris, 1867.

Irish Ecclesiastical Record, Dublin.

Laurin, J., Introductio in Corpus Juris Canonici, Freiburg, 1889.

Layman, Paulus, S. J., Theologia Moralis, Pataviae, 1723.

Leech, George L., The Constitution "Apostolicae Sedis" and the "Codex Juris Canonici," Washington, 1922.

Lehmkuhl, Augustinus, S. J., Theologia Moralis, Freiburgi Brisgoviae, 1910.

Leitner, Martin, Handbuch des Katholischen Kirchenrechts, Regensburg, 1922.

Leurenio, Petro, Jus Canonicum Universum, Venitiis, 1729.

Lijdsman, Bernardus, C. SS. R., Introductio in Jus Canonicum, Hilversum in Hollandia, 1924.

Maroto, Philippus, Institutiones Juris Canonici, Romae, 1921.

Martin, C., Omnium Concilii Vaticani Documentorum Collectio, Romae, 1873.

Muirhead, James, Historical Introduction to the Private Law of Rome, London, 1916.

Noldin, H., S. J., De Principiis Theologiae Moralis Oeniponti, 1921.

Noval, Josephus, O. P. Codificationis Juris Canonici Recensio-Historico-Apologetica et Codicis Piano Benedictini Notitia Generalis, Romae, 1918.

Noval, Joseph, O. P., De Judiciis, Augustae Taurinorum, 1920.

Perathoner, A., Das Kirchliche Gesetzbuch, Brixen, 1923.

Phillips, Georgius, Compendium Juris Ecclesiastici, Ratisbonae, 1875.

Pirhing, E., S. J., Ius Canonicum, Dilingae, 1674.

Pöschl, L., Kurzgefastes Lehrbuch des Katholischen Kirchenrechts, Graz, 1921.

Raus, P. J. B., C. SS. R., Institutiones Canonicae, Lugduni, 1923.

Reiffenstuel, Anacletus, Ius Canonicum Universum, Antverpiae, 1743.

Rezon y Fe, Madrid.

Roelker, E. G., Principles of Privilege According to the Code of Canon Law, Washington, 1925.

St. Thomas, Summa Theologica, Luxemburgi, 1890.

Scherer, Rudolf von, Handbuch des Kirchenrechts, Graz, 1886.

Schmalzgrueber, Franciscus, S. J., Jus Ecclesiasticum, Romae, 1845.

Schulte, Frederick, Geschichte der Quellen und Literatur, des Canonischen Rechts, Stuttgart, 1875.

Suarez, Franciscus, S. J., Opera Omnia, Parisiis, 1856.

Toso, Albertus, Ad Codicem Juris Canonici Commentaria Minora, Romae, 1921.

Vering, F. H., Lehrbuch des Kirchlichen, Orientalischen, und Protestantischen Kirchenrechts, Freiburg, 1893.

Vermeersch, A., S. J., Creusen, I., S. J., Epitome Juris Canonici, Mechlinae-Romae, 1921.

Wernz, Franciscus, S. J., Jus Decretalium, Prati, 1913.

Woywod, S., O. F. M., A Practical Commentary of the Code of Canon Law, New York, 1925.

Zallinger, Jac. Ant., Institutiones Juris Ecclesiastici, Romae, 1823.

DEUS LUX MEA

THESES

QUAS

AD DOCTORATUS GRADUM

IN

IURE CANONICO

Apud Universitatem Catholicam Americae

CONSEQUENDUM

PUBLICE PROPUGNABIT

NICOLAS JOSEPH NEUBERGER

SACERDOS DIOCESIS OMAHENSIS

IURIS CANONICI LICENTIATUS

HORA XI A. M. DIE XXVII MAII A. D. MCMXXVII

I. De Iure ejusque Divisionibus.
II. De Forma Regiminis Ecclesiae.
III. De Collectionibus Veteris Juris.
IV. Canones 1-5 De Iure non Tollendo.
V. Canon 6 De Relatione inter Ius Vetus et Codicem.
VI. Canones 8-16 De Legibus Ecclesiasticis.
VII. Canones 17-20 De Legis Interpretatione.
VIII. Canones 25-30 De Consuetudine.
IX. Canones 31-35 De Temporis Supputatione.
X. Canones 329-349 De Episcopis.
XI. Canones 350-355 De Coadiutoribus et Auxiliaribus Episcoporum.
XII. Canones 356-362 De Synodo Diocesana.
XIII. Canones 451-470 De Parochis.
XIV. Canones 471-478 De Vicariis Paroecialibus.
XV. Canones 487-491 De Natura et Divisione Religiosorum.
XVI. Canones 492-499 De Erectione et Suppressione Religionis, Provinciae, Domus.
XVII. Canones 518-530 De Confessariis et Cappellanis.
XVIII. Canones 531-537 DeBonis Temporalibus eorumque Administratione.
XIX. Canones 845-869 De Sanctissimo Eucharistiae Sacramento.
XX. Canones 871-892 De Ministro Sacramenti Poenitentiae.
XXI. Canones 893-900 De Reservatione Peccatorum.
XXII. Canones 901-907 De Subiecto Sacramenti Poenitentiae.
XXIII. Canones 951-967 De Ministro Sacrae Ordinationis.
XXIV. Canones 1006-1009 De Tempore et Loco Sacrae Ordinationis.
XXV. Canones 1012-1018 De Matrimonii Natura et Divisione.

XXVI. Canones 1023-1030 De Publicationibus Matrimonialibus.

XXVII. Canones 1035-1057 De Impedimentis in Genere.

XXVIII. Canones 1960-1965 De Foro Competenti in Causis Matrimonialibus.

XXIX. Canones 1974-1975 De Testibus in Causis Matrimonialibus.

XXX. Canones 1993-1998 De Causis Contra Sacram Ordinationem.

XXXI. Canones 2147-2156 De Modo Procedendi in Remotione Parochorum Inamovibilium.

XXXII. Canones 2157-2161 De Modo Procedendi in Remotione Parochorum Amovibilium.

XXXIII. Canones 2182-2185 De Modo Procedendi contra Parochum in Adimplendis Paroecialibus Officiis Negligentem.

XXXIV. Canones 2186-2194 De Modo Procedendi in Suspensione ex Informata Conscientia Infligenda.

XXXV. Canones 2195-2198 De Natura Delicti ejusque Divisione.

XXXVI. Canones 2199-2211 De Imputabilitate Delicti.

XXXVII. Canones 2220-2225 De Superiore Potestatem Coactivam Habente.

XXXVIII. Canones 2226-2235 De Subjecto Coactivo Potestate Obnoxio.

XLXIX. Canones 2236-2240 De Remissione Poenarum.

XL. Canones 2241-2254 De Censuris in Genere.

ROMAN LAW.

XLI. History.

XLII. Sources.

XLIII. Slavery.

XLIV. Citizenship.

XLV. Family.

XLVI. Adoption.

XLVII. Marriage.

XLVIII. Tutorship.

XLIX. *Capitis Diminutio.*
L. *Dominium.*
LI. Testaments.
LII. Possession.

INTERNATIONAL LAW.

LIII. Methods of Acquiring Territorial Jurisdiction.
LIV. Monroe Doctrine.
LV. Treaties.
LVI. Drago Doctrine.
LVII. Immunities and Privileges of Ambassadors.
LVIII. Prisoners of War.
LIX. Consuls.
LX. Extradition.

VIDIT FACULTAS:

PHILIPPUS BERNARDINI, S. T. D., J. U. D., Decanus.

H. LUDOVICUS MOTRY, S. T. D., J. C. D., a Secretis.

VIDIT RECTOR UNIVERSITATIS:
THOMAS J. SHAHAN, S. T. D., J. U. L.

BIOGRAPHY.

Nicolas Joseph Neuberger was born on December 1, 1897, at Stevens Point, Wisconsin. His primary education was received at St. Mary's School, Fond du Lac, Wisconsin. In June, 1919, he completed his secondary education at St. Francis Seminary, St. Francis, Wisconsin. In the Fall of the same year he entered Kenrick Seminary, Webster Groves, Missouri, where he pursued his philosophical and theological studies. In the Scholastic year 1924-1925 his bishop, the Most Reverend J. J. Harty, D. D., sent him to the Catholic University to enroll in the School of Canon Law, and to complete his theological studies at the Sulpician Seminary. On February 24th, 1925, he was ordained to the priesthood in St. Mary's Seminary Chapel, Baltimore, Maryland.

www.ingramcontent.com/pod-product-compliance
Lightning Source LLC
LaVergne TN
LVHW050158080826
844660LV00012B/311

* 9 7 8 0 8 1 3 2 2 2 3 3 2 *